James Thompson

VERONESE

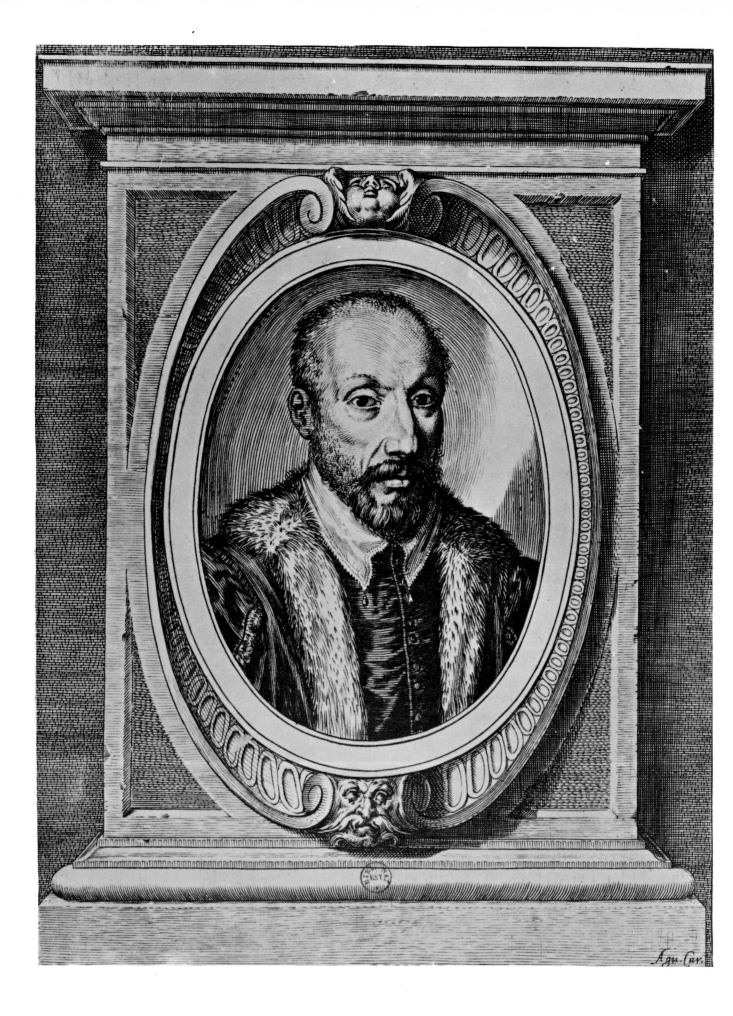

Agu. Car.

RICHARD COCKE

VERONESE

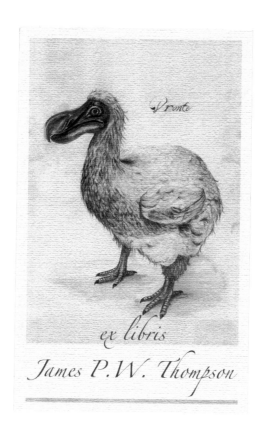

Vronte

ex libris

James P. W. Thompson

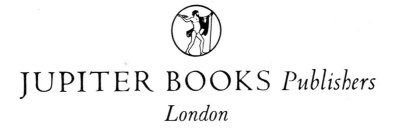

JUPITER BOOKS *Publishers*

London

Frontispiece
Paolo Veronese by Agostino Carracci. Engraving.

FOR SARAH

First Published in Great Britain by

JUPITER BOOKS (LONDON) LIMITED, 167 Hermitage Road, London N4 1LZ.

ISBN 0 906379 41 5

This book was produced in Yugoslavia

VERONESE

Veronese's paintings enjoyed an almost unchallenged reputation at least until the end of the nineteenth century; when in 1858 John Ruskin delivered his inaugural lecture as Slade Professor in the University of Cambridge he included a notable passage on *The Queen of Sheba before Solomon* in Turin (Plate 60): 'Well, one of the most notable characters in this picture is the splendour of its silken dresses; and in particular there was a piece of white brocade, with designs upon it in gold, which was one of my chief objects in stopping in Turin to copy. You may perhaps be surprised at this; but I must just note in passing that I share this weakness of enjoying dress patterns with all good students and all good painters . . . all the accessories are full of grace and imagination; and the finish of the whole so perfect that one day I was upwards of two hours vainly trying to render, with perfect accuracy, the curves of two leaves of the brocaded silk.'

Ruskin rightly evokes the staggering skill that we can find throughout Veronese's work, and this enthusiasm influenced the Pre-Raphaelites; but like other nine-teenth-century critics he was unaware of the way in which Veronese used his undoubted virtuosity to tell a story. The rich brocades of Sheba and her suite are part of the great sweep which leads up to the youthful Solomon enthroned to the left of the canvas; the com-position is very freely based upon an engraving by Marcantonio Raimondi (fig. 1) but the youthful Solomon has been substituted for the middle-aged figure in the print. This is an idealized reference to Charles Emanuel who had commissioned the canvas soon after his accession as Duke of Savoy in 1580, and the rich costumes embody the flattery of II Chronicles 9: 'happy are these thy servants which stand continually before thee'.

Veronese had been born Paolo Spezapreda, which means 'stonecutter', in Verona in 1528; his early train-ing is unclear, for his style, as we shall see, owes little to Badile or Caroto either of whom may have been his master. He was one of a generation of young painters, including Zelotti and Farinati among others, who were to follow the example of the more successful artists of the city and make their careers in Venice where he is first documented in 1555, having changed the family name to Caliari. Veronese must have moved to Venice because of the comissions offered for the redecoration of the rooms of the Council of Ten in the Ducal Palace (Plates 7 and 8) a project which brought him into contact with some of the most important members of the Venetian patriciate. Others from outside Venice participated in the redecoration, but, Veronese alone established him-self in Venice and the Veneto.

By the end of his career he was so successful that, as with Giovanni Bellini before him, he signed paintings which had been produced entirely by the workshop, which for a time at least continued after his death in 1588. Although his career can essentially be measured through his work for the Venetian patriciate, he was in contact with a wider clientele and early in the 1580s Philip II of Spain instructed his agent in Venice to see whether Veronese might come to work on the decora-tion of El Escorial because he thought Veronese to be a better painter than Federico Zuccaro with whom he was negotiating. He was right (as Zuccaro's dull work testifies) but unsuccessful with the aging Veronese.

Veronese's early work, from 1548 until roughly 1558, reveals his interest in contemporary Venetian art theory and the development of his interest in brocades around 1560 was a deliberate return to the tradition of Bellini and Carpaccio which, slightly later in the decade, is matched by a response to the demands of the Council of Trent, which itself leads to the sombre magnificence of the late paintings in the 1570s and 1580s.

The middle decades of the sixteenth century saw a new interest in artistic theory in Venice in the publica-tion of Paolo Pino's *Dialogue on Painting* in 1548, Doni's *Disegno* in 1549 and in Dolce's *Aretino, or Dialogue on Painting* of 1557. That some of these theoretical con-siderations were of immediate importance for Veronese is suggested by the earliest criticism of his work, that written by Francesco Sansovino, the scholar son of the great architect, in the first edition of his guide-book to Venice of 1556. He described Veronese's contribution to the redecoration of the rooms of the Consiglio dei Dieci in the Ducal Palace (Plates 7 and 8) as: 'opera veramente di disegno et gentile'. *Gentile* has a wide range of reference meaning both noble (as distinct from plebeian) and well and skilfully made. *Disegno* is the crucial term which the theorists connected with central Italian artists and whose absence in Titian's work was lamented by Vasari in his *Lives of the Artists* in 1550 and again in the 1560s.

Sansovino's use of the concept *disegno* for (Plate 8) recalls a now famous passage in Pino: 'if Titian and Michelangelo were of one body or if to the *disegno* of Michelangelo were to be joined the colouring of Titian

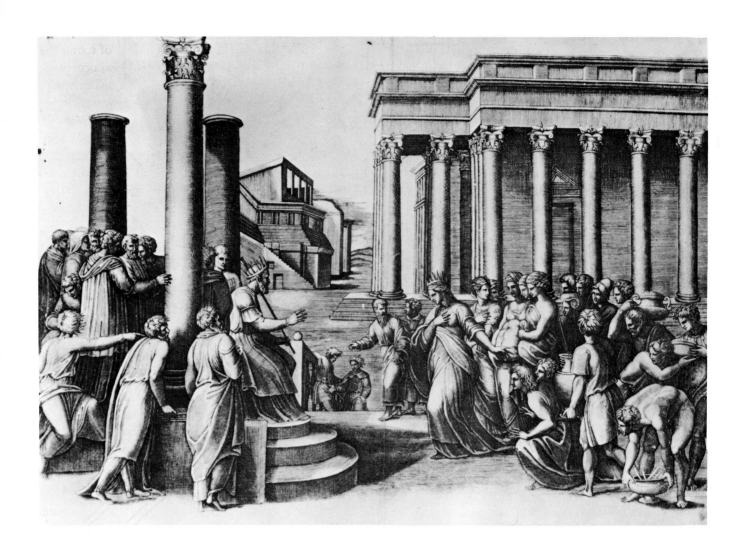

Fig. 1   The Queen of Sheba Before Soloman
Marcantonio Raimondi (after Peruzzi)
LONDON, British Museum, B. XIV 13, 13.

he could be called the god of painting.' Neither Pino nor Doni give a clear account of *disegno*, failing to emphasize either the range of drawings used in the preparation of a composition or the importance of drawing from the life. It is therefore not surprising that, although both Veronese and Tintoretto were inspired by the programme that Pino proclaimed, their working procedure and their style should owe more to Venice than to central Italy.

Veronese appears to have taken Pino's programme both literally, so that there are at least two drawings for his earliest painting the Madrid *Christ Preaching in the Temple* (Plate 1) of 1548 a rapid pen and ink sketch which owes much to Parmigianino and a chalk study for the scribe with a book at Christ's feet owing much to Titian's chalk studies, and in a general sense. His conception of history painting both in its use of gesture to characterize the scribes as they burrow in their books, and in the organisation of the details so that they never become obtrusive, derives from the central Italian tradition embodied in Marcantonio's engraving of the *Queen of Sheba* (Fig. 1) which may have been the source for the

relationship of the figures to the architecture as well as of the columns behind Christ.

This aspect of the *Christ Preaching*, which continues in the paintings of the 1550s, is matched by a treatment of colour that is Venetian both in the breadth of handling, which recalls that of mature Titian, and in the way in which it balances richness with a sense of narrative. In spite of the shadow created by his upraised arm, the pink of Christ's robe is the lightest tone in the canvas and hence the focus for the colour just as all the gestures and glances concentrate upon this figure.

Everything that we have said about the *Christ Preaching* underlines why it is so difficult to accept the traditional view that Veronese was trained by either Badile or Caroto whose efforts to assimilate sixteenth century sources were hampered by their sharp, harsh treatment of draperies, a continued legacy from the work of Mantegna which had had profound repercussions for painting in the city from about 1480 onwards. Here and in the next decade Veronese was to give the tradition springing from Mantegna renewed life for the palette in the *Christ Preaching* emphasizes yellows and greens in addition to pink in a way that is not found in Titian but which looks back to the range of colours that Mantegna employed in the *Triumph of Caesar*, which formed an outstanding part of the Gonzaga collection in Mantua.

The range of sources for the *Christ Preaching* continues in the paintings of the 1550s; the expressive torso of the tempter attacking the prostrate St. Anthony in the *Temptation* (Plate 4) of 1553 was suggested by Caraglio's engraving after Rosso Fiorentino's *Hercules and Cacus* and the elegant St. Catherine of the Giustiniani altar (Plate 3) derives from an etching by Parmigianino. The position of the Holy Family on the right of the canvas, the twin columns behind them and the high pedestal on which they are placed with the saints beneath reveal Veronese's study of Titian's great Pesaro altar whose colour he has followed more closely than before (Fig. 2). The vigorous twisting Fame in the *Time and Fame* (Plate 2) of the same year, 1551, reveals his interest in Giulio Romano, an interest that was to mature in the great decorative achievements at S. Sebastiano and Maser, (Plates I, II, 9–12, 14–19). The complex foreshortened St. Paul in the *Conversion of St. Paul* (Plate 5) derives from the Laocöon but the changes in the pose and costume suggest that, like Tintoretto, the figure was studied from a model. Although undated the overcrowded action of the *Conversion* does not fit with later pictures; the energetic leaping horses that distract attention from the fallen saint anticipate those in S. Sebastiano (Plate I) and derive (although with much greater energy and movement) from a facade on the Corso in Verona which had a traditional attribution to Mantegna.

The fleeing horse in the background accompanied by a servant has been studied from Raphael's cartoon of the *Conversion* which was then in the Grimani collection in Venice. The interest in Raphael resulted in a now lost copy after the *Madonna della Perla* which is now in Madrid but which in the middle of the sixteenth century was in the Canossa collection in Verona; this study influenced the elegant swirls of the Virgin's drapery in the *Coronation of the Virgin* (Plate 9 and Fig. 3) with which Veronese began the decoration of S. Sebastiano late in 1555. The light, rather unusually bright colour is very different from the heavy shadows of the Raphael and the poses of the Virgin and of Christ look back to earlier Venetian versions of this subject. The decorative panels around the central rectangle are filled with cartouches and rich swags which derive from engravings after the school of Fontainebleau and which anticipate the later development of Venetian ceiling frames.

Veronese achieves a new complexity of pose in the foreshortened St. John the Evangelist who looks up to witness the Coronation in heaven above his head; the pose suggests the example of the Sistine ceiling (notably the Jonah) (Fig. 4) which he may have seen before painting the ceiling of the sacristy at S. Sebastiano. According to an old tradition he visited Rome together with Girolamo Grimani; Grimani was *capo* of the Consiglio dei Dieci in 1555, one of the three years that he visited Rome, and it is reasonable to assume that he

took with him on this trip the young Veronese who was then involved in the decoration of the suite of rooms in the Ducal Palace that the Consiglio dei Dieci occupied (Plates 7 and 8). The paintings of the following years (Plates 6 and 7) reveal Veronese's new awareness of Roman painting; the monumental Age in the *Youth and Age* (Plate 7), for instance, fuses the pose of the Daniel on the Sistine ceiling with the head of Ezechiel and the discrepancy between the steep angle at which the seat is viewed (notable in the step) and the much flatter handling accorded the figure recalls Michelangelo's ignudi.

We have lost earlier illusionistic ceilings from the Ducal Palace, destroyed by fire, but the freedom with which the figures move in the great *Jove Expelling Crimes and Vices* (Plate 8) suggests the majestic freedom with which Michelangelo invested God the Father in the history scenes in the second half of the Sistine ceiling (from the *Creation of Adam* to the altar) rather than any Venetian precedent. The firmness with which the figures in Plates 7 and 8 are modelled recalls Sansovino's choice of epithet for these canvases: *disegno*; this, however, is only half the story for the *disegno* is combined with a rich play of light and shade and with the contrast between the white clouds and the brilliant blue sky.

The rooms in the Ducal Palace are small when compared with the nave of S. Sebastiano (Plates I, 10–12) for which Veronese produced one of the most splendid decorative ensembles of the sixteenth century in 1556 and 1557. Venetian ceiling design had been given a new impulse in the early years of the previous decade by Titian's great ceiling in Santo Spirito which has now been removed to the sacristy of S.M. della Salute. Titian conveyed the drama through the enormous figures, sombrely lit in front of dark skies which open in the *Sacrifice of Abraham* to underline the presence of the Holy Spirit, an allusion to the dedication of the church.

As with other Venetian ceilings the complex heavy gilded frame was already in position establishing the contrast between the central square (Plate 11) and the two flanking ovals (Plates I and 10) and calling for the smaller canvases which flank the main narrative scenes. In these smaller scenes Veronese has brilliantly reinterpreted the illusionistic oculus of Mantegna's Camera degli Sposi in the Ducal Palace at Mantua with sharply foreshortened balustrades on top of which vigorous small angels support garlands. The grisaille figures in the corners besides the oval canvases look back to the spandrel figures on Roman triumphal arches, but those by Veronese are handled with a vigour and liveliness that had eluded his collaborators at the Ducal Palace.

As with Titian Veronese has taken the spectator into account so that the ideal viewpoint for the central *Coronation of Esther* (Plate 11) is as one enters the church from under the monks' barco and that for the *Triumph of Mordechai* (Plate I), which is towards the altar, is from under the *Coronation*. The spectator could not look up

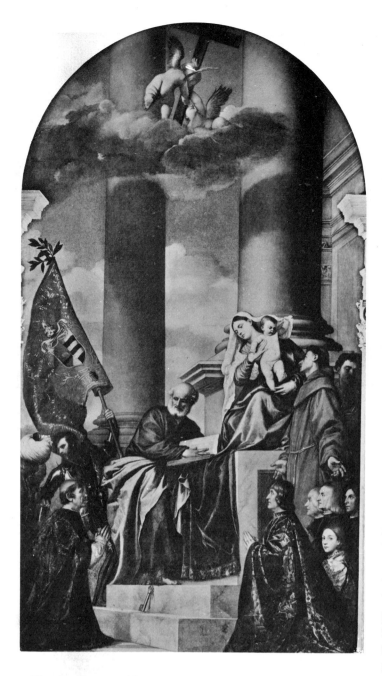

Fig. 2 Pesaro Altar
Titian
VENICE, Frari.

directly at the first canvas in the series, the *Esther Brought Before Ahasuerus* (Plate 10), because of the monks' *barco* and this canvas is therefore turned on its axis so that it is viewed from the centre of the church (under the *Coronation*) with the spectator's back turned to the altar.

The colours, especially after the restraint of Titian, are striking with the emphasis upon greens, reds and yellows, which are strongly reminiscent of Mantegna's *Triumph of Caesar*. The colour is not, though, an end in itself (although this is the impression that you will get if you are unfortunate enough to see the ceiling by the artificial lights that are installed and which upset the balance); in the *Coronation* (Plate 9) Esther's green robe

isolates her and helps to focus attention upon her as does the light red of Mordechai's robe in the *Triumph* (Plate I), which is carefully differentiated from that of the flag of the Empire which is waved so prominently to the right.

Contemporary Venetian art-theorists, notable Dolce, greatly admired foreshortening and the bravura of the *Triumph* must have excited enthusiasm for the horses leaping down at the spectator, a reworking and simplification of those in the *Conversion of St. Paul* (Plate 5). The soldier leading Mordechai's horse leans back in a pose that was suggested by Michelangelo's Jonah on the Sistine ceiling so that we see Mordechai's head and shoulders behind him; the soldier is in shadow and the pale red of his cloak seems to focus attention on Mordechai. This is as close as Veronese ever comes to virtuosity for its own sake; in one of the three roundels that he painted for Sansovino's library in the following year (Plate 13) the pose of the soldier is repeated in the lady standing with her ledger-book but the complexity of the *Triumph* has been abandoned.

The other notable innovation in these ceilings is the steeply foreshortened architecture within which the figures are set with such confidence; the formula looks back to the ceiling of the Sala di Psiche in the Palazzo del Te in Mantua which had been decorated by Giulio Romano. Giulio, however, was only able to work on a small scale compared with the very large surfaces that Veronese filled with such assurance and the foreshortening in Giulio's ceiling lacks the unfailing certainty that we find at S. Sebastiano.

The scheme was completed by frescoes initially in the upper part of the church and then (some time later) the twelve apostles in the nave. The scheme of the upper part brilliantly complements that of the ceiling so that to the spectator in the nave the foreshortening of the twisted columns echoes that of the balustrade (Plate 12). Such a scheme goes back to a now lost decoration in the Mantuan Ducal Palace by Giulio Romano which had been brought back into prominence in Venice by the Rosa brothers who painted a, now lost, set of illusionistic columns on the ceiling of the Madonna dell'Orto.

That the Venetian patriciate admired these skills is witnessed by the decoration of Villa Barbaro (Plates II, 14–19) which Veronese completed probably in the late 1550s for Marcantonio and Daniele Barbaro (Plate 20). Both appear to have been interested in the arts; Marcantonio collaborated with Veronese on a now lost cycle of paintings and Daniele besides producing in 1556 the edition and translation of Vitruvius that he holds in the portrait had been the author of the programme for the rooms of the Council of Ten (Plates 7 and 8). The brothers' villa was designed by Palladio but they must have suggested the vaulting in the *salone* which they intended for Veronese's great suite of frescoes where the illusionism of the slightly earlier frescoes at S. Sebastiano is developed with a new and unsurpassed

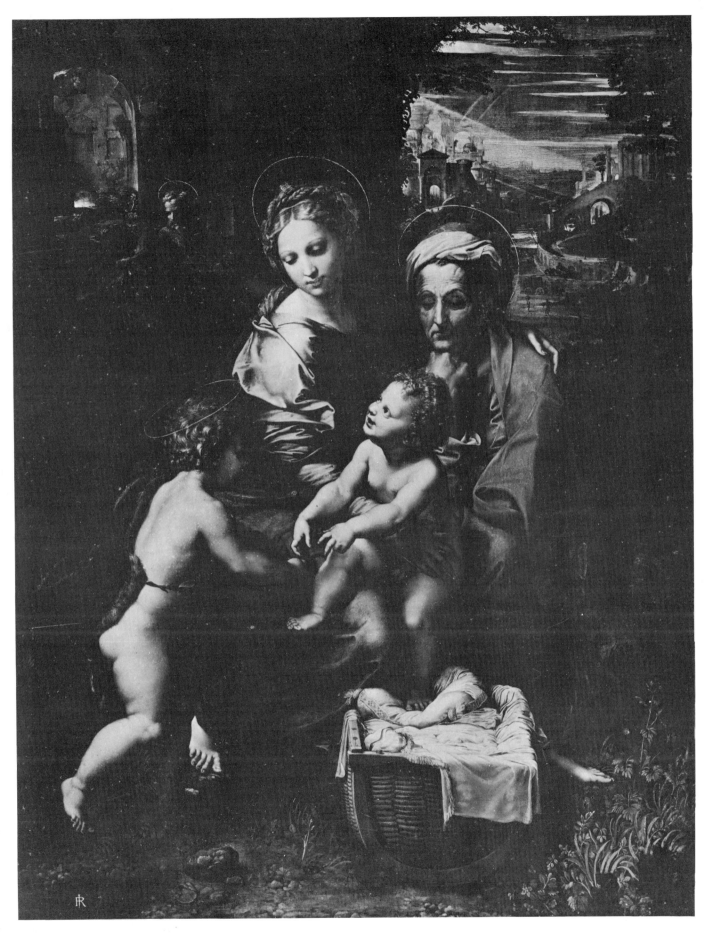

Fig. 3   Holy Family with St John the Baptist (the Perla Madonna)
Raphael
MADRID, Museo del Prado.

9

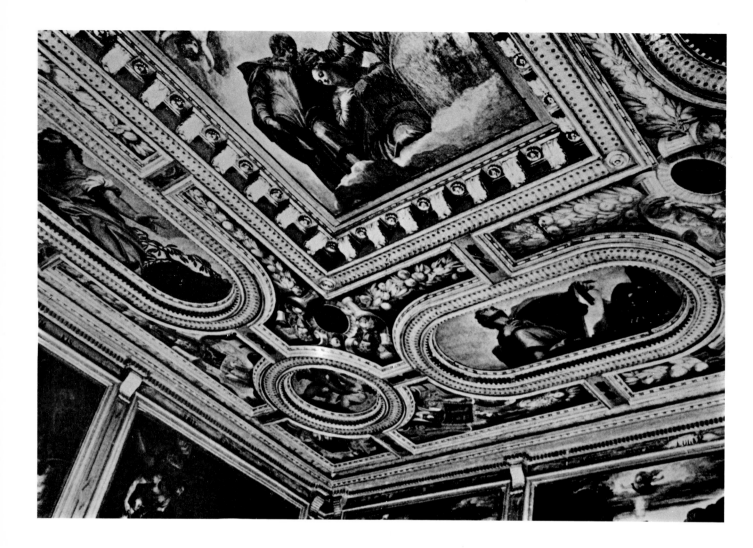

**Fig. 4 View of the ceiling of the sacristy,
S. Sebastiano**

richness and inventiveness. Veronese has again taken
account of the direction in which the frescoes were to be
viewed. Unlike the modern spectator the early visitors
to the villa would first visit the nymphaeum to the north
of the *salone* where the fresco cycle begins with a lady
whose attributes identify her as Felicitas Publica (the
public good) which establishes the Barbaros' concern
for the public domain; they would then walk into the
salone (Plate II) where they would be greeted by the
lady in the centre of the ceiling riding her great snake.
She is probably Thalia surrounded by the planetary
gods in their normal zodiacal houses with the four
elements in the fields outside the great central octagon.
This frame, which is an elaborate reworking of a type
that the Renaissance had developed from one of the
stucco ceilings in Hadrian's villa at Tivoli, is supported
on the two side walls by foreshortened twisted columns
which lead down to the main cornice.

A balustrade runs round the room above the cornice
and on one side a mother, nurse and small boy look at
the spectator while on the other a monkey perches on
the balustrade while two boys hold a book and a dog,

symbols of learning and the hunt, both of which were
enjoyed by the villa's inhabitants. On the walls (Plate
14) Corinthian columns set on a richly marbled dado
support the cornice and frame the niches in which Peace
and Faith view the ceiling; on the longer walls the
columns frame landscapes which, with the exception of
the crossing (Plate 17) continue on the walls of the other
four rooms that Veronese frescoed (Plates 15, 16, 18 and
19).

The landscapes evoke both the foothills of the alps
where the villa is set and also a poetic vision of a roman-
tically ruined Rome, which is a final tribute to the
backgrounds of Mantegna's paintings where a passion
for archaeology is combined with a love of ruins. Five of
the landscapes are based upon the views of Rome by the
Flemish engraver H. Cock, a reflection of the interest of
the patrons for Daniele Barbaro had visited Rome together with Palladio. Where Cock accurately records
the ruins in their contemporary setting Veronese replaces the modern buildings with an imaginative series
of ruins; the changes indicate that the landscapes which
relate to engravings by another artist from Verona,
Battista Pittoni, do not derive from the engravings but
served as Pittoni's inspiration.

Landscape had long played an important part in the
decoration of Renaissance villas but those at Maser re-

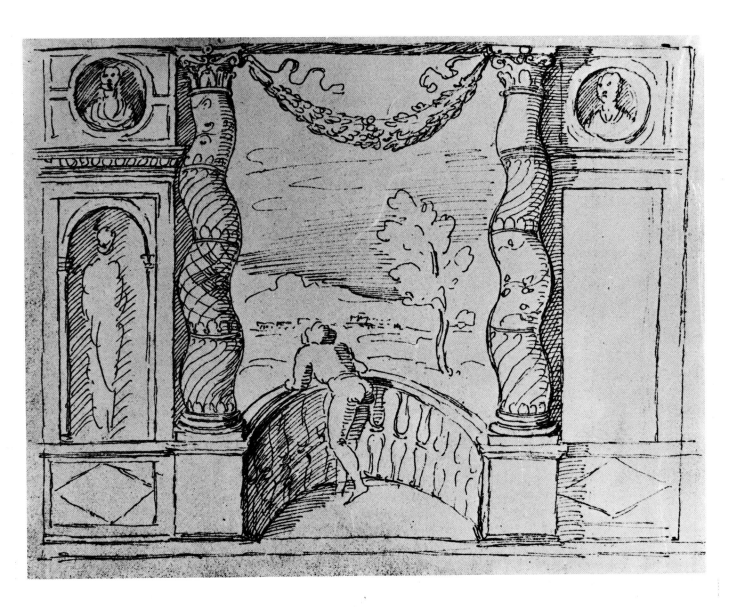

**Fig. 5 Sixteenth century copy after a lost
decoration in Mantua by Giulio Romano**
Anon.
BERLIN.

call in their range—with harbours, ruined theatres,
palaces, villas (including a distant view of Maser in the
salone) and small figures going about their work—Pliny
the elder's description of the landscapes of Studius: 'He
introduced a delightful style of decorating walls with
representations of villas, harbours, landscape gardens,
sacred groves, woods, hills, fishponds, straits, streams
and shores, any scene in short that took the fancy. In
these he introduced figures of fishers, or of fowlers or of
hunters or even vintagers. He also brought in the fashion
of painting seaside towns on the walls of open galleries,
producing a delightful effect at very small cost.'

The invention that marks out the landscapes is also
found in the frames in which they are set; the scheme
has its origin in now destroyed frescoes by Giulio
Romano recorded by an anonymous Flemish visitor to
Mantua in the sixteenth century (Fig. 5). Veronese has
given greater depth to his wall, introduced a greater

range of textures with coloured marble, cameos and
swags and varied both the orders between the rooms and
also the way in which the columns frame the doors and
windows. There is a splendid series of jokes including
the apparent curve to the frame of the wall in the Stanza
della Lucerna (Plate 16), the mock classical statues to
the sides of the landscape in that room and the small
painted portraits that we appear to glimpse next to a
statue in the Stanza di Bacco (Plate 19).

The rich profusion of this invention is linked with a
programme: Daniele Barbaro wrote in his annotation to
chapter V of Book VII of Vitruvius that: 'Painting
should have an intention and represent an *effetto*, and all
the composition should be based on the *effetto*, and like
fiction painting should be useful and like music it should
have a design.' In the *salone* (Plate II) we have already
noted the planetary gods in their zodiacal houses surrounded by the four elements with a lady riding a snake
in the centre; the Renaissance concept of the harmony
of the spheres would link together these disparate
figures, provide a reasonable identity for the lady in the
centre (Thalia, the ninth muse) and connect the room
with the eight ladies in the crossing (Plate 17) whose

musical instruments thus identify them as the remaining muses.

The Barbaros would have been well familiar with the idea that the musical harmonies are in-born in man because they reflect the harmony with which the planets move. The great Florentine neo-Platonist Marsilio Ficino had, at the end of the fifteenth century, attempted to correlate the nine musical modes with the seven planets and this was taken up by Francesco Gafurius at the beginning of the sixteenth century who had added an extra planet and subtracted one of the muses (Thalia) to get the scheme to work.

Veronese's version of this subject is infinitely more successful and classical than the rather charming wood-cut that accompanied Gafurius' *Practica Musice* of 1496; it is not the only theme in the room, let alone the villa, but it had the attraction of being a general *effetto* of the type that Barbaro demanded for painting. This same complex of ideas is further reflected in the ceiling of the Stanza di Bacco (Plate 18) where Bacchus appears both as the god of wine pressing the grapes out into the cup held by his huntsmen and also as the leader of the muses whose music soothes the melancholic genius resting wearily on his left arm.

In his brilliant realization of this complex programme Veronese drew upon a wide range of sources. The grouping of the planetary gods and Thalia suggest the influence of Correggio's cupola of the *Vision of St. John the Evangelist* in S. Giovanni Evangelista, Parma where there is a comparable break between the foreshortened apostles and the central figure. The individual figures both here and in the rest of the villa reveal the influence of the antique as it had first been interpreted by Raphael; the connection with Raphael is important both for individual motifs and also for the elegant restraint with which Raphael approached the antique, which had been abandoned by the younger generation of central Italian artists in their search for *maniera*.

The combination of a relief-like grouping with rolling clouds in the lunette of Venus and Vulcan at the top of Plate 14 recalls Raphael's *Marriage Feast of Cupid and Psyche* in the Farnesina, although Veronese avoids the illusion of a tapestry and where he re-used the scheme on a ceiling (Plate 18) was prepared to foreshorten the figures. Both the Venus on the ceiling of the Sala dell' Olympo and the Providence in Plate 15 derive from the Grace with her back to the spectator in Raphael's lunette of *Cupid with the Three Graces*, although Veronese also reveals his knowledge of the antique Crouching Venus that inspired his immediate prototype. This knowledge of the form of the Roman gods is combined with an instinctive feeling for the correct mood for the figures. The rather grumpy Neptune on the ceiling of the Sala dell' Olympo is accompanied by a playful putto lifting a huge shell while another plays with one of Juno's birds tied to a piece of string. Venus in the centre of the ceiling has confiscated Cupid's bow and arrows

and has made him write out his alphabet, Diana caresses one of her dogs who places an affectionate paw in her lap and Mercury holds his caduceus, the symbol of his eloquence. At his feet a putto holds an astrolabe which indicates Daniele Barbaro's interest in astronomy, which he was careful to distinguish from astrology which he believed to be meaningless.

We have no direct comment upon Maser by either of the patrons (and Palladio also fails to mention the decoration in his account of the villa in the *Four Books of Architecture* of 1570) but later they are said to have recommended Veronese for a share in the decoration of Sala del Maggior Consiglio in the Ducal Palace that was destroyed in the fire of 1577. We can get an indirect measure of Veronese's success from the passage in Daniele's edition of Vitruvius in which he notes that painters should be skilful in elegant poses and foreshortening, graceful outlines (*contorni*) flesh painted with *morbidezza*, the proper expression of mood rank etc and differentiation between male and female nudes. These terms were the common currency of Venetian critical thought of the late 1550s but looking back at Villa Barbaro we see this, and much more, in Veronese's frescoes.

It is not surprising that Daniele Barbaro should choose to have his portrait painted by Veronese (Plate 20); Barbaro had been painted by Titian about ten years earlier but he might well have agreed with a later visitor to Venice, Sir Philip Sidney, who wrote in 1574 about the decision to have his portrait painted saying that he was undecided between Tintoretto and Veronese: 'who hold by far the highest place in the art.' The choice went to Veronese and a year later one of Sidney's friends wrote about that, now lost, portrait: 'The painter has represented you a little sad and thoughtful.' This is the mood that is captured in the portrait of Barbaro, probably painted around 1556, where the learned cleric is shown seated at a table holding open various pages of his 1556 edition of Vitruvius. The column to the right is a further indication of his interests, but one that is not allowed to distract from the sitter; although there is little new in this or the other portraits by Veronese, he handles the accepted formulae with skill and sensitivity to the sitter. There is a considerable range from the use of attributes here and in the *Portrait of Alessandra Vittoria* (Plate 49) to the straightforward presentation of the Woman in Plate 21 where the precision of the costume is combined with a feeling for her presence. The sculpture on the marble base and the view of St. Mark's in the distance must once have identified the now anonymous man in Plate 22; his casual contraposto as he leans against the ledge from which spring the twin columns framing the statue influenced Rubens' Genoese portraits and hence one aspect of the Baroque portrait.

The support and interest of Daniele Barbaro may also have been important for the growth of Veronese's interest in brocades and rich fabrics that become such a feature of his paintings in the 1560s (Plates III and IV); the usual perspective in which Venetian critics viewed Renaissance painting was the essentially Vasarian one of progress: poor old Bellini got so far before being overtaken by Giorgione and Titian. The manuscript of Daniele Barbaro's *Treatise on Perspective*, published in 1569, included a passage which although it did not find its way into print, suggests that he did not altogether share this view. In his discussion of the vanishing point he states that as a general rule it should be on a level with the heads of the main figures; it can be higher when the things shown are lower than the level from which they are viewed, as in Bellini's lost Naval Battle, or when it is the reverse it can be lower as in Mantegna's Eremitani chapel frescoes.

Barbaro's mathematical interests lead him to admire a type of painting which others had found outdated; Veronese, as we have seen, must have been predisposed to share this view since he was himself interested in Mantegna. One other factor may have influenced the rich sunlit brocades that we find in the saints on the outside of the organ shutters from S. Geminiano (Plate 25) of 1558 to 1561; Dolce, writing in 1557, had commented on the monotony of the graceful mannerist style and Veronese may have turned to the tradition of Bellini and Carpaccio as a way of avoiding the pitfalls of the current central Italian style.

Those other great organ shutters, which were added somewhat belatedly to the upper nave of S. Sebastiano (Plate 26), illustrate the skill with which Veronese paints in the style advocated by Daniele Barbaro. The viewpoint of the *Presentation* is low and the blending of painted pilaster and real corinthian column reflects the link that Mantegna had established in the S. Zeno altar in Verona. The colonnade that runs behind the figures when the shutters are open for the *Pool of Bethesda* reflects the painted cornice that runs behind the figures in the Mantegna; just as the forms that Veronese employs betray his awareness of the current architectural vocabulary so his figures are painted with a breadth and fluency that we find in the sixteenth but not in the fifteenth century.

The composition is a good example of the skill with which he reconciles the demands of narrative with an interest in rich effect. The figures are composed in a deep frieze-like grouping which is maintained in the front plane; the great curving arch that frames the figures is masked at its lower springing so that the apparent depth of the building is denied. Veronese achieves a flowing rhythm through the line of heads which, like the glances of the attendants, focuses attention upon Christ who is set off by the brilliant blue of the Virgin's robe which is the main accent of the colour in both canvases.

While the compositional devices of the *Presentation* recur in the Turin *Feast in the House of Simon* (Plate 27),

in the *Martyrdom of St. Sebastian* (Plate 34) and in the great series of *Adoration of the Magi* (Plates 43 and 44) it is, perhaps, difficult not to agree with Sir Joshua Reynolds' classification of Veronese as a decorative painter, when faced with the *Marriage Feast at Cana* (Plate 30). In his fourth *Discourse* of 1771 Reynolds attacked Veronese as follows: 'The subjects of the Venetian Painters are mostly such as give them an opportunity of introducing a great number of figures. I can easily conceive that Paul Veronese, if he were asked, would say that no subject was proper for an historical picture, but such as admitted at least forty figures; for in a less number, he would assert, there could be no opportunity for the painter's showing his art in composition, his dexterity of managing and disposing the masses of light and groups of figures.'

Reynolds would have been surprised to find that his heroes, the Carracci, greatly admired Veronese who played a crucial part in the development of Annibale's style in the 1580s. Blinded as he was by his dislike of the contemporary Venetian revival of Veronese, he failed to appreciate that the 'managing and disposing of the masses of the light' plays an integral part in the narrative. We can begin to appreciate this by looking at the photomontage (Fig. 6) which replaces the picture on the end wall of the refectory of S. Giorgio Maggiore under Palladio's great cornice. This cornice is echoed in the balustrade in the centre of the canvas, above Christ's head, which cuts off the sixty or so guests in the foreground from the servants behind. It also shows how the rich marble doric columns in the foreground with their entablature topped by a balustrade do not echo the line either of the cornice on the long walls or of the windows. The break with the real space of the room, which is caused by placing the vanishing point of the architecture in Christ's head, draws attention to three groups in the foreground: the small page on the left who offers a glass of wine to the host of the Feast watched by a grand servant with his foot on the step and another who rests from pouring; the group of musicians in the centre (Plate III) dominated by Christ; the servant in the beautiful brocade standing contemplating a glass who is behind a servant pouring out the water and in front of the monks, who are in shadow.

The traditional way of showing the miracle in the *Marriage Feast* is by emphasizing the servants pouring great stone jugs of water into elegant wine pitchers. This moment, John 2, 1–10, was retained when in the sixteenth century the *Feast* became isolated from cycles of the life of Christ as a subject for a refectory. Because of the scale of his painting Veronese has combined this moment with the slightly later one: 'And he (Christ) saith unto them, Draw out now and bear unto the governor of the feast. And they bare it. When the ruler of the feast had tasted the water that was made wine and knew not whence it was: (but the servants which drew the water knew)'.

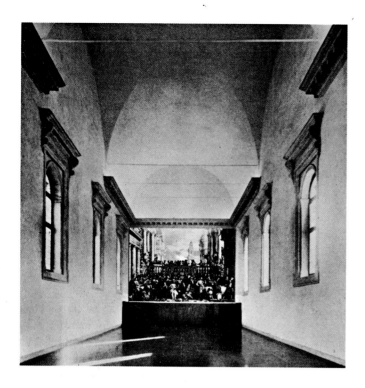

Fig. 6 Photomontage of the Marriage Feast at Cana in the refectory of S. Georgio, Maggiore Venice

The servants in the foreground invite the spectator to share their wonder at Christ's miracle and the musicians, who include Veronese and Titian, must be understood as celebrating Christ's power. This awareness of the miracle fills the foreground while the superb detail—guests wiping their faces with their napkins or picking their teeth—is in the background, a background whose importance is diminished by setting the recession of the tables higher than that of the architecture, above the head of Christ.

Critics are often tempted (understandably) to compare this vast canvas with the theatre and there is indeed something theatrical in the modern sense about the richness of the costumes and setting. It is, however, a mistake to claim that the Renaissance theatre helped Veronese visualize this scene for the sixteenth century saw the development of two traditions of theatre design, neither of which appears relevant to the *Marriage Feast*. The roman architect Peruzzi and his follower Serlio designed elaborate illusionistic settings according to the nature of the play (tragic, satyric or comic) which are more concerned with recession than the setting of the *Feast*; the alternative tradition was embodied in Palladio's *Teatro Olimpico* in Vicenza where the action is set in front of a *frons scenae* reminiscent of a triumphal arch. Neither tradition influenced the *Feast* where the massive columns which frame the figures open onto a vista of sky in a way which influenced baroque stage design, notably that of the Venetian Giacomo Torelli; it is because of this influence that Veronese's works appear to us theatrical.

The style of the *Feast* marked a return to the Venetian

tradition of Bellini and Carpaccio; its appeal was not confined to a Venetian clientele for the *Omnia Vanitas* and the *Honor et Virtus Post Mortem Floret* (Plates 37 and 38) were probably commissioned for the elector of Bavaria, Albrecht V, in 1567. These canvases, together with a number of outstanding mythological paintings (Plates 39 and 40), share the rich costumes, warm light and frozen movement of the *Feast*; the Frick paintings differ from the others in their programme, which is proclaimed by the inscriptions on the canvases. In Plate 37 Christian Truth's faith in God is contrasted with the world's baubles and with the melancholic gaze of Hercules and in Plate 38 the young man who must (following the inscription) be Honour, embraces Virtue and flees from death on the left with nothing worse than a tear in his stockings. The pictures demand a specific context, unlike the other canvases, which may have been the marriage of Albrecht's son and subsequent heir, Wilhelm V, which the Bavarian court celebrated with ostentatious expense in 1568.

The Frick paintings share the classicism of Maser, where the planetary gods are based upon Roman models, most notably in the Hercules of Plate 37 who is based upon the famous Roman Hercules in the Farnese collection, Rome. Mercury in the *Mercury, Herse and Aglauros* (Plate V) derives from a well-known Roman type both in his figure and attributes, the winged hat and caduceus; the picture shows the climax of the story in Ovid's *Metamorphoses* where the jealous Aglauros tries to stop Mercury from visiting her beautiful sister Herse and he turns her to stone. The choice of moment has suggested a series of visual puns; Mercury and Aglauros resemble a group of sculpture, but sculpture whose life is underlined by setting them in front of the statue in the niche.

The sense of tragedy is lost in the richness of the setting (itself suggested by the Ovidian text) and the restrained gesture with which Herse witnesses her sister's fate; this same cheerfulness recurs in the *Mars and Venus* (Plate 39) in New York where Venus is shown after bathing, her robe hung over the bower behind her while Cupid joins her to Mars. Venus presses her breast and the milk that spurts as a symbol of the fertility of their union is echoed by the water running from the lion's mouth; Venus smiles down on Cupid as he ties the lovers together and another putto bears off the sword that Mars will not need for some time. This cheerful mood also prevails in the potentially much more erotic small *Mars and Venus* (Plate 40) in Turin; at last both lovers are undressed (itself rare in Veronese) but they are interrupted by Cupid leading Mars's aimable horse down the steps to peer into the room.

It is hardly surprising that the *Rape of Europa* (Plate 41) painted in 1573, should eschew the drama and pathos of Titian's version of this subject and return to the older tradition of book illustration to show Europa attended by her companions sitting shyly on the bull's back. Veronese's sense of decorum meant that he never exploited the landscape-style of Maser (Plate 19) in his easel-paintings; the screen of trees framing the foreground figures and opening up to allow a vista of Europa carried away by Jupiter marks the development of a formula for landscape that was to recur in the 1570s (Plate 64). Europa and her companions are notable both for their costumes and for the fluency with which the figures are linked, a fluency that is repeated in the Adoration of the Magi (Plates 43 and 44) with equally rich costumes.

The pyramid in the background proclaims Veronese's care for the Ovidian text which specified that the scene was to be set in Phoenicia; this makes the apparent incongruities in the Family of Darius before Alexander (Plate VI) all the odder. Alexander wears stunning red classical armour but both of his companions are in contemporary armour and the setting is also wrong for the encounter after the battle of Issus should take place in the country, perhaps in front of a tent. These discrepancies are all the more striking in view of the care which has been taken with the depressed servants on the left and with Darius' mother who is not subservient in her plea to Alexander. The choice of moment gives a guide to the sense in which the picture is to be read; Veronese has depicted not the usual moment of Alexander's magnanimity but that which accompanied it when Darius' mother mistakes his companion Hephaestion for Alexander but is put at ease by Alexander saying that Hephaestion is another Alexander. Together with the discrepancies in armour and the setting this must be intended to underline a contemporary reference and although we do not know who commissioned the painting it is tempting to speculate that it may have been Pietro Pisani who had fought in Dalmatia in 1570, when he is said to have captured more than a thousand turks, a feat worthy of another Alexander.

The range of allusion that we found in the mythologies is repeated in the religious paintings where they link with some of the major religious movements of the period. The S. Zaccaria altar (Plate 31) of the early 1560s echoes Bellini's altar in the nave of the church in the decorated pilaster, the strip of sky to the left and the richly ornamented cloth of honour behind the Virgin. The composition is a variation on that of the S. Francesco alla Vigna altar (Plate 3) which shows a greater command of the brush in evoking a wide range of textures; both the gestures and the colour link the saints more closely with the Holy Family than previously and this emphasis comes into focus when we remember that the picture was commissioned by Francesco Bonaldi and commemorated Jerome and John Bonaldi.

By contrast the saints in the main altar of S. Sebastiano (Plate 32) are thrown into shadow by the brilliance of the heavenly vision of the Virgin and Child accompanied by music-making angels. The contrast between the saints in shadow and the Holy Family in the light, which is not found in the picture's source, Titian's altar from S. Nicolò now in the Vatican, establishes a set of priorities for the saints through whom the spectator experiences the vision, which links with one aspect of the Council of Trent's decree on the veneration of saints and their images.

This devotion had been challenged by Luther in 1522 and his call to ban images from churches was eagerly taken up by the Calvinists through whose influence it began to take effect in France in the early 1560s and the Netherlands from 1566. Calvinist iconoclasm, which was hardly an issue in Italy, was only brought to the attention of the Council of Trent in November 1562 through the intervention of the French who wanted a policy of accommodation with the Calvinists. The Council's decree issued on the 3rd of December 1563 followed closely a slightly earlier French document in its emphasis on the images of saints as exemplars, to be followed by clergy and congregation alike. But the decree also reaffirmed that the invocation of saints was not idolatrous: 'but good and useful because their intercession is effective through Christ our only redeemer and saviour.'

Veronese would have been well informed about the Council's proceedings for as Patriarch elect of Aquileia (the costume in which he is depicted in his portrait Plate 20), an older see than that of Venice, Daniele Barbaro had played an important part in the Council's considerations in the early 1560s. The Virgin and Child Appear to SS. Anthony and Paul (Plate 28) of early 1562 shows why he was responsive to this aspect of the decree. The saints are usually shown alone in the wilderness and there is no literary source for the appearance of the Holy Family; the contrast between the shadow of the earthly sphere and the light of the heavenly vision, the low viewpoint and St. Anthony's rapt devotion anticipate the saint's role as intercessor which finds its fullest expression in the great Martyrdom of St. George (Plate 35) most probably painted in 1566. The attendants, the horsemen, the priests and the idol are traditional elements that derive from earlier martyrdoms (Plate 34) but they are grouped around the saint so that they do not distract from his still prayer as he ignores the priest urging him to worship Apollo. His plea as he looks up to the heavens is received by the Holy Family through the intercession of SS. Peter and Paul together with Faith, Hope and Charity while an angel carries down the martyr's palm and laurel.

The emphasis upon the saint as intercessor breaks with the tradition both for St. George and for other saints and establishes a new type of martyrdom that Veronese re-used in the Martyrdom of St Justina (Plate 47) and which influenced artists as different as El Greco and Elsheimer. The, comparative, peace and stability of Italy in the 1560s, which contrasts with the religious persecution and martyrdom of both Catholic and Calvinist common in the rest of Europe, helps to explain why the calm stillness of the saint in Plate 35 is so very different from the bloodshed and torture found in later paintings influenced by the decree of the Council of Trent, but which reflect the sufferings of the Jesuit order.

The calm security of late sixteenth century Venice is suggested by the *Mystic Marriage of St. Catherine* (Plate IV) where the red drapery around the twin columns and the saint's beautiful brocade with a pattern of gold, blue and yellow on white convey a festive mood, which is taken up by the choir of angels accompanied by the lutenists. This celebration of the saint's vision (the basis for the subject), which is here developed for the first time in the Renaissance, and the burst of golden light in which the martyr's crown and palm are borne down draw the spectator to share in the mystic marriage.

This view of Veronese as an artist responsive to the spirit of Catholic reform embodied in the Council of Trent must appear difficult to reconcile with his appearance before the inquisition on 18 July 1573 to answer a series of questions about the *Feast* (Plate 46). Most modern scholars believe that the original subject of the *Feast* was a *Last Supper* both because this was the subject of the Titian which it replaced and because the text refers to it as an: 'ultima cena'. The text is not an exact transcript of what was said but a shorthand précis of the proceedings and it seems unlikely that it was ever intended as the same subject as the (admittedly later) *Last Supper* (Plate 63). One of Veronese's first replies when asked whether he knew why he was there was: 'I was told by the Reverend of the Fathers, that is the Prior of SS. Giovanni e Paolo, whose name I do not know, that the inquisition was here and that you illustrious gentlemen had ordered me to paint the Magdalen in place of a dog, and I had replied that I would be glad to have done this and anything else for my honour and that of the painting, but that I did not think that a figure of the Magdalen could be added convincingly'. The Magdalen anointing Christ's feet is the central moment in the *Feast of the House of Simon* (Plate 27); we can speculate that since he had already painted three *Feasts in the House of Simon* with this scene (two quite recently in Venice) the original contract, which has not come down to us, may have called for him to vary his treatment of the theme, which would explain the intervention of the inquisition.

That remains guess-work; but his appearance contains a coherent defence of the painting in terms of its decorum that modern critics appear to have overlooked in their emphasis on Veronese as an unlearned painter. When he was questioned about the servant wiping his nose and the soldiers he argued: 'the patron of the house was, as I have been told, grand and rich and should have such servants' (such a host plays no part in the gospel account of the *Last Supper* but is central to the *Feast in the House of Simon*). When the subject arose again Veronese strengthened his case by observing that the offending figures are: 'outside the place where the feast is held'.

The triple division of the canvas by the Corinthian columns and the smaller Serliana echoes the division of the cornice; Christ in the centre of the canvas is emphasized by making the central arch wider than those at the side and by being the only figure framed by the sky (the others are set against the distant view of a city). Some servants are inside the main part of the building but the figures to whom the inquisition objected are either in front of the columns or on the stairs that lead to the central opening, a device that he had first used the year before in the *Feast of St. Gregory the Great* (Plate 45).

The defence, which supports our view of the skill with which Veronese arranges his compositions, is better than the alternative that he was following the precedent of his betters, for the example which he cites of the unsuitability of Michelangelo's nude *Last Judgement* was rejected by the inquisition. He had also claimed the licence allowed to poets and 'matti', an abbreviation that is usually taken to mean mad-men; such a claim would itself appear lunacy before the inquisition where the maximum penalty was death by drowning and I think it more likely that he meant mathematicians. This would make the licence that Veronese claimed close to that of Aristotle's *Poetics*: 'saying what can happen in a strictly probable or necessary sequence', which would fit with his friendship with the distinguished Aristotelian and mathematician, Daniele Barbaro.

At the end of Veronese's appearance it was noted that he should: 'change the painting so that it would be suitable as an *Ultima Cena*.' This did not happen; instead, by a compromise not suggested in the text, the title was changed to that of the *Feast in the House of Levi* with whose action as described in Luke it hardly fits for no scribes or pharisees rebuke Christ.

One of those entitled to sit on the tribunal with the inquisitor was the Patriarch of Venice, since 1560 Giovanni Trevisan, who later in the decade commissioned the *SS. John the Evangelist, Peter and Paul* (Plate 53) for his church. S. Pietro in Castello. This fact alone shows the consideration which Veronese continued to enjoy among the influential patriciate in Venice some of whom must have worked for the compromise adopted in the *Feast*.

As befits an altar commissioned by Giovanni (John) Trevisan St. John is placed above SS. Peter and Paul; the saints are not set in an architectural framework but in a romantic landscape and the aura of mystery is heightened by the sombre tonality and by the angel appearing in a burst of light to St. John who holds aloft the chalice, one of his attributes. The picture has been transformed from the conventional *sacra conversazione* by the memory of Carpaccio's *Agony in the Garden* in San Giorgio degli Schiavoni; the change may well have been prompted by the Catholic defence of the sacrament of the Eucharist which had been challenged by Luther's view that it was only a sign, that Christ was not present and that the sacrament should not be adored. The reaction had begun in Milan in 1527 with the non-liturgical worship of the host in the services of benediction, in the forty hours' exposition which was much popularized by the Capuchins and Jesuits and which was fully endorsed by the twenty-third session of the Council of Trent.

The devotion shaped the planning of Tintoretto's decoration in the Sala Grande of the Scuola di S. Rocco in the later 1570s and influenced a number of other paintings by Veronese including the *Doge Sebastiano Venier's Thanksgiving for the Battle of Lepanto* (Plate 51) where the chalice held by Faith is placed prominently under Christ's left foot. It must also have played a part in the choice of subject (and of its treatment) for the main altar of the church of S. Giacomo (St. James), the *Christ with Zebedee's Wife and Sons* (Plate 54); St. James, shown as a man with his pilgrim's staff, is in the centre of the canvas while his mother presses the suit for her children to sit on Christ's left and right and he enquires: 'Are you able to drink of the cup that I shall drink of, and to be baptised with the Baptism that I am baptised with?'

The eucharistic chalice borne high above the altar by two angels and blessed by God the Father anticipates the elaborate settings for the non-liturgical worship of the host that were developed early in the seventeenth century. The devotion influenced not only public works but also the smaller *Martyrdom and Last Communion of St. Lucy* (Plate 65), intended for private use; the priest with the host is given a prominence not found in Altichiero's frescoes of the life of St. Lucy in Padua, which Veronese would have known. The efforts to put the saint to death had been to no avail (they included dragging her round the city with the oxen which are shown in the background) until she was ministered the rite of communion.

The brooding character of the *Martyrdom of St. Lucy* is exaggerated by its rubbed condition but like many late Veronese's it was thinly painted, partially as a response to the sketchy quality of late Tintoretto, and it is one of a number of paintings which reflect Tintoretto's influence through which Veronese learned to vary the style of his work according to the subject matter. The attendants, the elegant steps on which the saint is posed and the rich brocade of the robe in the 1575 *Martyrdom of St. Justina* (Plate 47) continue the style of the 1560s; the light effects in the upper part where the dark figures of the Dëesis are contrasted with the burst of light behind them look back to Tintoretto's *Last Judgement* in the Madonna dell'Orto (Fig. 7). The figures in the *Apostles* (Plate 48), painted at the same time and for the same city, are more dramatic, the range of colour more subdued and the effect more intense than in the *Martyrdom*; here, and in the other paintings which

reflect his interest in Tintoretto, the poses are never so exaggerated, the range of colour is wider and the pictures are more finished.

The commission in 1583 to paint an *Annunciation* (Plate 59) for Philip II of Spain must have recalled his patronage of Titian and the dramatic gesture with which the angel greets the Virgin looks back to Titian; but the setting with its balustrade, God the Father appearing with the heavenly host in the burst of light show his independence as does the colour with the flickering yellow highlights on the angel's pale pink costume. Another Titian, the *Portrait of Jacopo Strada* (Plate VIIIa), with whom as we have already seen (Plates 37 and 38) Veronese was in contact in 1567 (the date of the portrait), provided the model for the *Judith* (Plate VIII). The fashionable garments, the elegant hair, the string of pearls around her neck, the chain and arm-band do not, like the costume of Hollywood stars, distract from her appearance as a heroine, which is realised through the sombre tonality broken by the pale blues of the costume and by the certainty with which she moves to her right while looking back at the maid on her left.

For the King of Spain Veronese used the more 'public' style that we find in the contemporary *Queen of Sheba before Solomon* (Plate 60) and in the later work in the Ducal Palace (Plates 50–52) which had been ravaged by fire in 1574 and again in 1577; it was as a result of this latter devastation that the Sala del Maggior Consiglio had to be redecorated with the grandiose series of ceiling paintings which culminated in the *Venice Triumphant* (Plate 52) above the Doge's throne. According to a late, but reliable, tradition the three members of the commission responsible for the scheme had to approach Veronese to undertake the work; this is plausible both because of the amount of work that he appears to have had in hand and because of the freedom that he was allowed. The manuscript with the commissioners' scheme has survived and while Veronese has fulfilled the demand for the figure of Venice: 'enthroned in imitation of Rome seated on the globe crowned by Victory' the allegorical figures no longer accompany Victory but sit at Venice's feet. The allegories follow closely those of the scheme but the four putti who represented the four seasons have been abandoned; instead the idea of the contentment of the people is realised in the crowd behind the balustrade looking up at Venice. The soldiers and their captives who are not mentioned in the scheme, must have been included by the artist to fit with the other paintings of the ceiling.

The scheme makes no mention of the magnificent setting with the great foreshortened triumphal arch and twisting columns which, together with the rich contrasts of light and shade, show the development since the ceilings of S. Sebastiano (Plates I, 9–12). The crucial change, that the space is defined by the architecture rather than by the figures, had first occurred in the

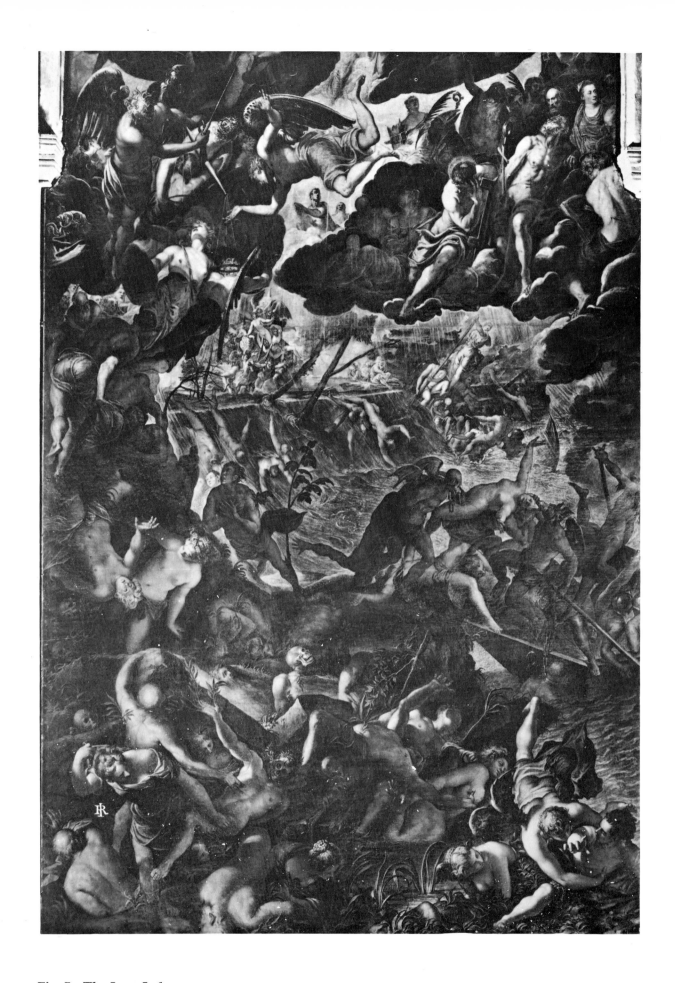

Fig. 7 The Last Judgement
Tintoretto
VENICE, Madonna Dell'Orto.

Assumption of the Virgin (Plate 36) of the 1560s. In its energetic gestures and in the red of the Virgin's mantel trailed by the angels and set off against the golden heavens it reflects Titian's *Assumption* in the Frari, but the virtuoso architecture suggests a transposition of one of the bays of the Sistine ceiling seen by the spectator with his back to one of the long walls in the chapel. The Evangelist in the foreground has replaced the prophet and the steps and balustrade leading to the sarcophagus equal the prophet's throne; the remaining apostles are in the position of the ignudi with the Virgin and her attendants substituted for the central history.

The growth of Veronese's response to the text can be seen in the late *Crucifixion* (Plate 57) where the dark skies, which dominate the canvas, are offset by the pale women framed by the rearing horse, an interlude that underlines that Christ is the focus of the colour and the light. The gestures underline Christ's primacy and the incidental details, the dead rising from the grave, the spectator fleeing in terror, are in the shadowy foreground. The choice of Matthew 27, although not without precedent, must have been made to contrast with Tintoretto's huge *Crucifixion* in the Sala dell'Albergo of the Scuola di S. Rocco. This great altar inspired a number of versions of which the most dramatic is the superb canvas in Budapest (Plate VII); although not a narrative picture it conveys great emotion through the deep greens of the sky which set off the glittering aureole around Christ, whose head falls forward at the moment of death.

The intensity of these religious paintings recurs in the late mythological paintings, the *Venus and Adonis* and the *Cephalus and Procris* (Plates 61 and 62), for instance. They were painted as a pair in the early 1580s and while this is not the first example of this practise (see Plates 37 and 38 for example) Veronese uses the contrast to establish a pessimistic view of life. The pictures complement each other with framing trees to left and right, in the figure groups—in one the young man lies in the woman's lap in the other the woman is cradled by the man—and in mood. Although darker than the earlier mythologies the pale red of Adonis's costume establishes the mood for the lover's idyll which contrasts with the dark shadows in the *Cephalus* which echo the tragedy of the story. The choice of subject underlines these contrasts, for Venus warns Adonis of the dangers of hunting, dangers that are embodied in the tragedy of Procris's death at the hands of her huntsman husband.

The simplification of the landscape and the sombre range of subdued greens recur in the *Christ with the Woman of Samaria* (Plate 70) which is probably one of Veronese's last paintings. The drama of Christ's long dialogue with the woman of Samaria is expressed by his outstretched left hand as he asks her to draw water for him; the apostles in the centre of the canvas on their return from shopping do not distract from the calm eloquence of the foreground figures. The simple settings of these canvases contrasts with the more complex landscape of the near-contemporary *Baptism* (Plate 58) which combines the Baptism with the Temptation which follows it in the gospels; the complex thick woods on the left and the exposed middle ground on the right (all of which were to influence Annibale Carracci) suggest the desert far from Jerusalem whose appearance above the trees in the background is crucial for the Temptation.

Veronese died in April 1588 and it is perhaps no accident that two of his last paintings should be concerned with divine healing; the saint in the *St. Pantaleon Heals a Sick Boy* (Plate 68) turns and looks up at the angel through whose power he has just driven out the small demon from the sick boy held by the parish priest. The saint is emphasized both by the pyramidal grouping and by the brilliant red of his costume, which is clearly not contemporary, and the herm on the right establishes late antiquity as the period of the miracle; the dim broken buildings in the background recall Dürer, in whose settings Tintoretto had shown renewed interest. In the *Deësis with SS. Roch and Sebastian* (Plate 69) the saints, the Virgin and St. John intercede with Christ on behalf of the city in the middle distance with an intensity which is a vivid testimony to the ravages of the plague. The Virgin and St. John have been developed from those in the upper part of the *Martyrdom of St. Justina* (Plate 47) with an expressive *contrapposto* that is also found in the St. Sebastian, whose pose is more dramatic than that of his immediate source, the St. Sebastian in Plate 51.

These qualities were not lost upon a younger generation of artists and Annibale Carracci's reform of painting in Bologna would not have been possible without the example of Veronese. One of the Carracci, probably Agostino, wrote in their copy of the 1568 edition of Vasari's *Lives*: 'I have known Paulino and I have seen his beautiful works. He deserves to have a great volume written in praise of him, for his pictures prove that he is second to no other painter, and this fool passes over him in four lines, just because he wasn't a Florentine.' The praise is echoed in Annibale's paintings which set a pattern that was to be followed in the seventeenth century by giving the figures more bulk and weight, bringing them closer to the surface of the canvas and working out the landscape with a new sense of depth. The influence and the praise continued until the 1660s when Bernini on his visit to Paris revived Vasari's prejudices against Venetian painting and applied them to Veronese. This prejudice may well reflect the change in taste in Roman painting as Maratta and Gaulli grew away from an interest in Venetian painting but it was not shared by the French Academie where in 1667 Le Nôtre emphasized the nobility of the *Supper at Emmaus* (Plate 23) the quality of the drawing, the variety of the heads and their decorum.

It is precisely this awareness of the link between Veronese's virtuosity and the narrative that Reynolds destroyed in the *Discourse*, part of which we quoted on page 00. Reynold's view was prejudiced by his dislike of Sebastiano Ricci who had rediscovered Veronese in 1708; Ricci, and following him Tiepolo, saw in Veronese bright colour, rich but unhistorical costume and grand patrician figures all of which they accomplished with a free, decorative brush-stroke. Interest in Veronese was strengthened, rather strangely, by the enthusiasm for the true expression of Christian sentiment at the beginning of the nineteenth century, which helped to shape Ruskin's admiration for the *Queen of Sheba before Solomon* (Plate 60), an admiration to whose limitations we have already alluded. Although the Pre-Raphaelites shared Ruskin's interest Veronese's influence seems confined to some of their late work, while the interest which Turner and Delacroix expressed in their writings is not reflected in their paintings.

This fits with a wider change in the historian's view of Venice; Burckhardt's account of the Renaissance, published in 1860, with its emphasis upon the equality of the classes, the enjoyment of festivals, the development of the individual and the emancipation from religion became part of the romantic picture of the city that stems from Molmenti's account of Venetian private life, published in 1880. This account of Venetian society has been challenged by recent social historians who emphasize the intellectual life of the nobility, their important role in the Catholic reform movement, the skill with which the state adapted the *scuole* to accommodate the orders excluded from the highest offices and the city's continued commercial prosperity through to the beginning of the seventeenth century. This changed perspective should help us to accept that Veronese was, for all his limitations, an artist with a wider range and a more serious view of painting than is commonly acknowledged.

BIBLIOGRAPHICAL NOTE

The most accessible volume is that prepared by R. Marini, with introduction by G. Piovene, in the Classici dell'Arte series, Milan, 1968. Professor Pignatti has compiled a much fuller, and much more expensive, volume, *Veronese, L'Opera Completa*, 2 Vols., Venice, Alfieri, 1976. I have indicated some articles which may be of interest in the Notes on the Plates, but J. Schulz *Venetian painted ceilings of the Renaissance*, Berkeley 1968 and W. Wolters, *Plastische Deckendekorationen des Cinquecento in Venedig und im Veneto*, Berlin 1968 are two specialized studies which are worth consulting.

Note to the Plates

In the dimensions height precedes width; all the pictures are oil on canvas unless otherwise stated.

The following abbreviations are used:

B.M.   *Burlington Magazine*

A.B.   *Art Bulletin*

J.W.C.I.   *Journal of the Warburg and Courtauld Institutes*

M.X.I.F.   *Mitteilungen des Kunsthistorischen Institutes in Florenz*

M.D.   *Master Drawings*

P.   *Pantheon*

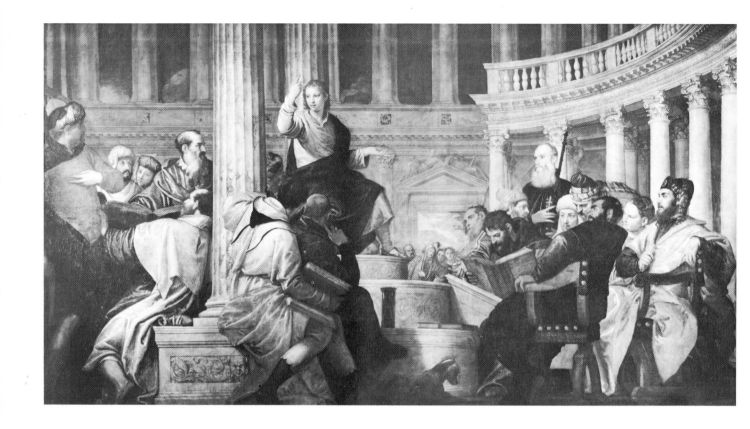

1 Christ Preaching in the Temple

MADRID, Prado. 236 × 430 cm.

The picture, which is dated: 'MDXLVIII' on the book held by the man seated beneath Christ, was painted when Veronese was only twenty years of age. The scene is set in a striking evocation of the Temple of Jerusalem with Christ raised on the steps as he expounds the scripture; his parents enter in the background in search of their son while the scribes look surprised or burrow in their books, and behind them stands the otherwise unidentified donor with a red cross of Jerusalem embroidered on his black cloak. The picture departs from the tradition of Dürer's woodcut of this subject, which was the model for the painting by Bonifazio de' Pitati, the most distinguished Veronese artist of the older generation, now in the Palazzo Pitti, Florence; for all the fluency of the composition it lacks the coherence that Veronese was to achieve in his mature paintings. The picture was first recorded in the Spanish Royal collection in the Salon de los Espejos in the Alcázar in 1686, whence it subsequently passed to the Prado*. The date which was first noted by Michael Levey, B.M., 1960, pp. 106 ff, is not accepted by many Italian scholars but there seems little reason to doubt it. Preparatory drawings for the canvas were discussed in the B.M., 1971, 726 ff. A version of this subject, which is dated 1576, forms a part of the series of seven canvases illustrating scenes from the life of the Virgin in the Ateneo Veneto, Venice. It is one of those that have been claimed for Veronese but like the others in the series is, I believe, a product of the workshop.

* See Bottineau, *Bulletin Hispanique Bordeaux*, 1956 and 1958.

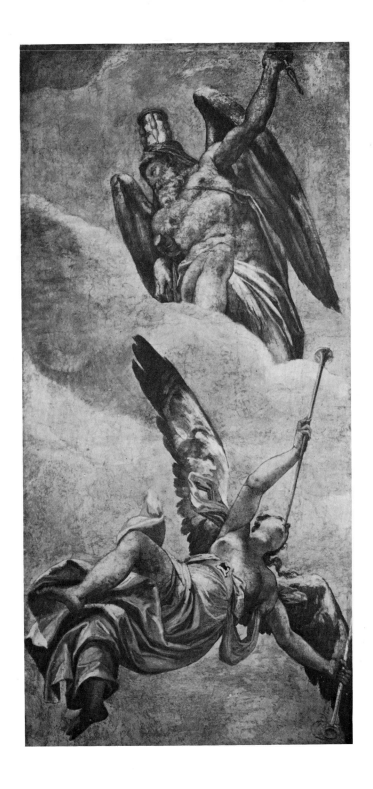

2 Time and Fame

CASTELFRANCO, Duomo. 353 × 168 cm. Fresco removed to canvas.

Time is identified by the hour-glass on his head, his wings and his crutches and Fame by her two
trumpets and wings. Time's pose, which derives from that of the Laocoon, is handled with none of
the foreshortening of the later *Jove Expelling* (Plate 8) and it suggests the example of Giulio
Romano's *Laocoon* in the Sala di Troia in the Palazzo Ducale just as the swirling pose of Fame
derives from the angels which Giulio had designed to support the Virgin's crown of Twelve Stars in
the Cathedral, Verona. The fresco is one of the fragments, possibly from the salone, of the
decoration of Villa Soranza undertaken by Veronese and Zelotti in 1551 (the date of the *Fame* in
the Seminary, Venice); the fragment was one of those removed to canvas by Filippo Balbi in 1816,
the date of the destruction of the villa, and subsequently given to the Cathedral by Balbi who sold
the bulk of the work in London, G. Schweikhart, M.K.I.F., 1971, 187 ff. For a preparatory drawing
for *Fame* see M.D., 1973, 138 ff.

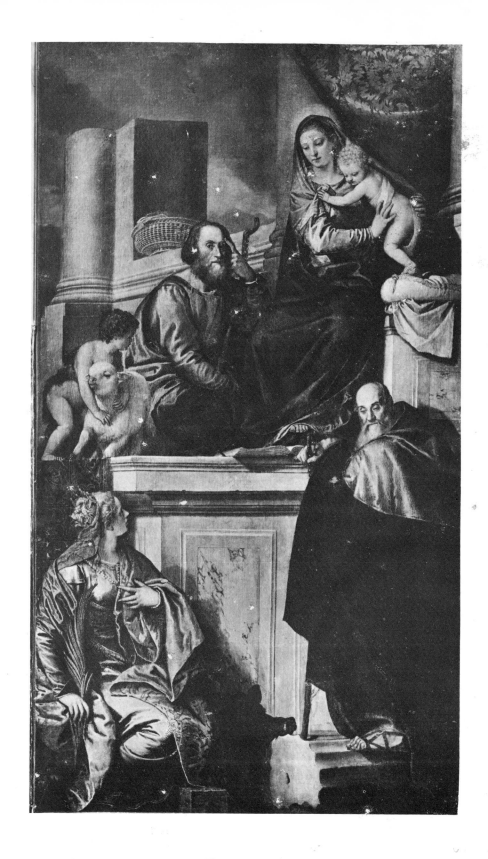

3 Holy Family Enthroned with John the Baptist, SS. Anthony Abbot and Catherine

VENICE, S. Francesco alla Vigna. 313 × 190 cm.

The composition develops that of Titian's Pesaro altar but the elegant St. Catherine, identified by the fragment of the wheel on which she rests her feet, reflects an interest in Parmigianino. The picture completed the decoration of the fifth chapel on the left which had been conceded to Lorenzo Giustiniani in 1536 and was built by 1543. An inscription refers to the dedication of the chapel to Antonio and Lorenzo Giustiniani in 1551; this is the probable date of the altar whose figures and their relationship to the architecture fit with that of the *Christ Preaching* (Plate 1) but lack the sophistication of the drapery style of the 1555 *Coronation of the Virgin* (Plate 9).

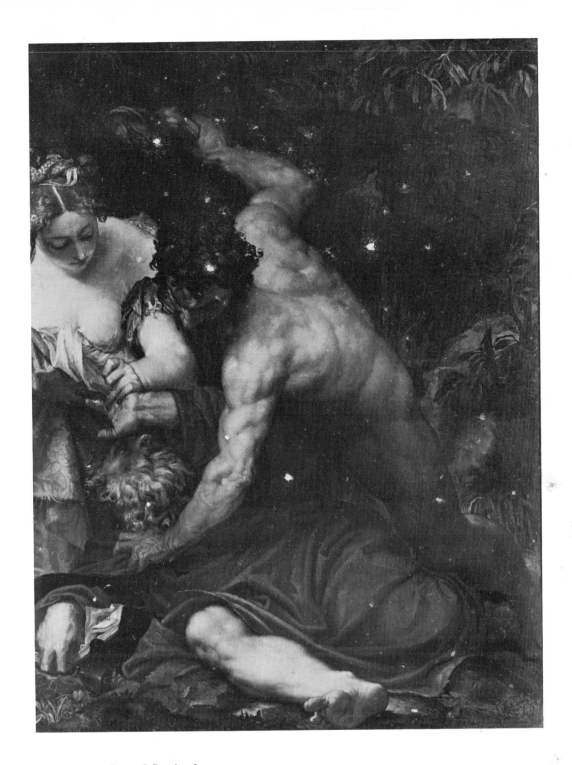

4 Temptation of St. Anthony

CAEN, Musée des Beaux-Arts. 198 × 151 cm.

The agonized saint and the female temptress about to dig her fingers into his hand reflect the St. Jerome and the Virgin in Parmigianino's *Virgin and Child with SS. John the Baptist and Jerome* in the National Gallery London. The tempter derives from Caraglio's engraving after Rosso's *Hercules and Cacus* (see B.M., 1971, 726 ff.); the ultimate source of the figure is Michelangelo's *modello* in Casa Buonarotti which also inspired Tintoretto's *Cain Slaying Abel* now in the Accademia, Venice of 1553. The picture was one of a series of canvases painted for the Cathedral, Mantua between 1552 and March 1553 at the commission of Ercole Gonzaga. The other Veronese artists who took part were Domenico del Moro, Paolo Farinato and Domenico Brusacorci; the scheme was completed by Fermo Ghisoni, Costa and G. M. Bedoli and the whole commission was probably the responsibility of G. B. Bertani. The picture, which has been cut down slightly, was removed on Napoleon's order in 1797, sent to Paris and thence to Caen in 1801. The drawing of this subject in the Louvre (Rosand, B.M., 1966, p. 421) is not, in my view, a preparatory sketch for the painting but is one of a number of early independent chiaroscuro drawings.

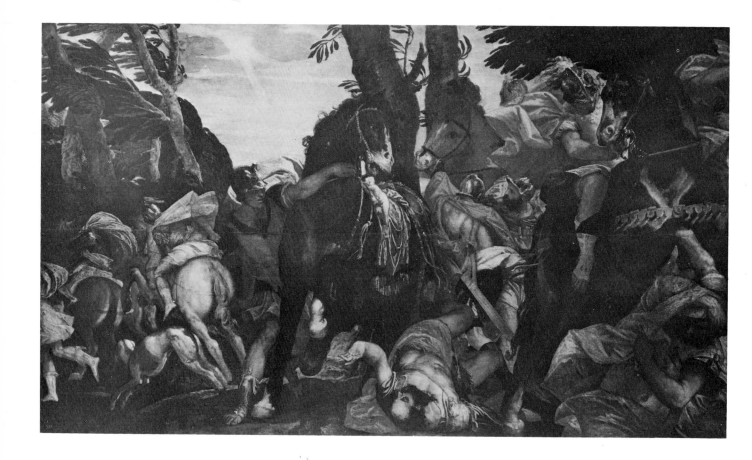

5 Conversion of St. Paul

LENINGRAD, Hermitage. 191 × 329 cm.

The *Conversion* had long afforded artists an excuse to display their mastery over rearing horses, a tradition that had been introduced to the Veneto by Jacopo Bellini in his sketchbooks and continued by Pordenone in a now lost painting which is known through a drawing (exhibited, Morgan Library, New York, 1965, no. 53). The combination of the rearing horse on the right, a motif with a distinguished history in the Renaissance, with the Saint's horse raising its left leg to avoid trampling on St. Paul recalls the fresco on Niccolò Giolfino's house in Verona which had an old, but not necessarily reliable, attribution to Mantegna (see B.M. 1972, 322 ff.). Although often dated to the end of Veronese's career the awkwardness of the composition and the close links with the *Triumph of Mordechai* (Plate I) where the same motifs are used with greater feeling for the story, suggest an early date for this picture whose early history before its acquisition from Gatschina Palace in 1920 is not known.

(opposite)

6 Transfiguration of Christ

MONTAGNANA, Duomo. 535 × 250 cm.

The composition with Christ, Moses and Elias on the mountain with the apostles below goes back to a Byzantine tradition which Giovanni Bellini had re-interpreted in his painting in the Museo Correr, which influenced Pordenone's 1511 version now in the Brera, Milan; the great cloud and the figure of Christ derive from Raphael's *Transfiguration* then in S. Pietro in Montorio, Rome. The frame, behind the main altar, which was built in imitation of that of Titian's *Assumption of the Virgin* in the Frari, was completed in 1554. The contract for the painting was signed in the villa of Francesco Pisani on the 3rd June 1555 and the picture was due for completion by Christmas 1556. Daniele Barbaro (Plate 20) was one of the canons at Montagnana and may have been responsible for giving the comission to Veronese.

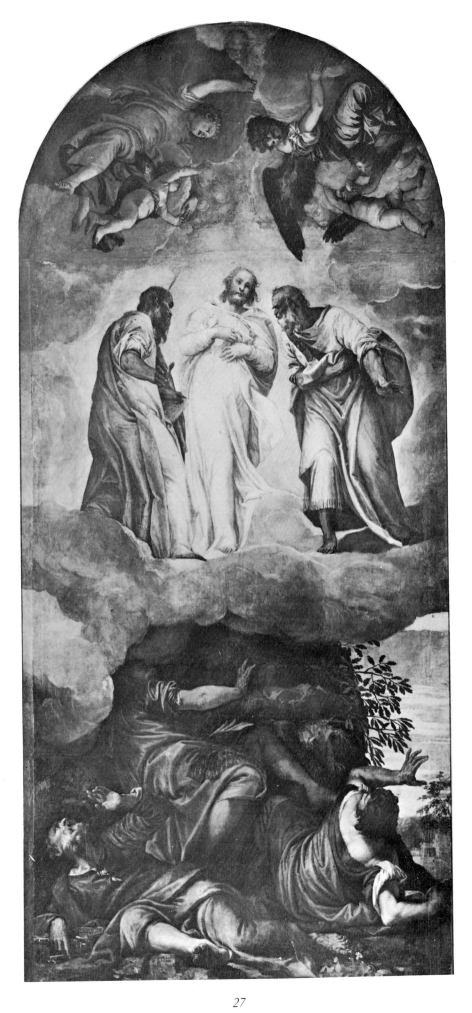

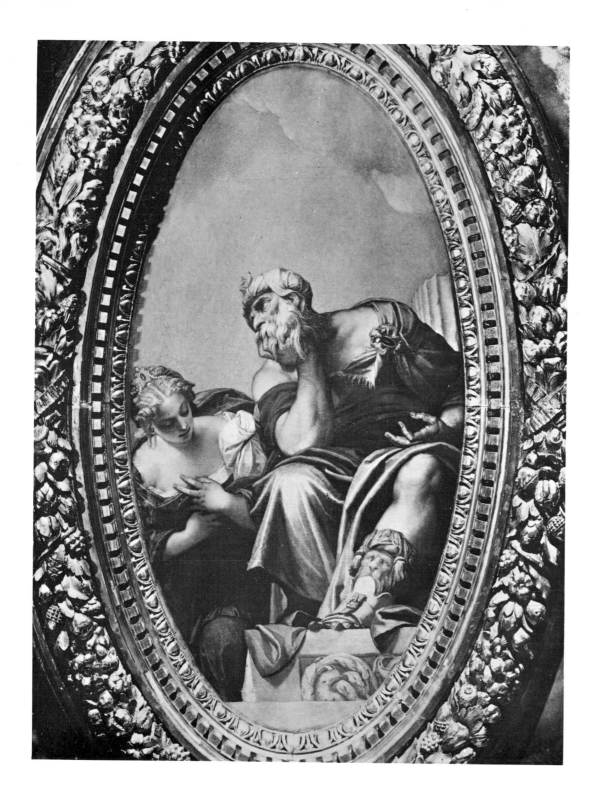

7 Youth and Age

VENICE, Ducal Palace, Stanza del Consiglio dei Dieci. 280 × 145 cm.

The meaning of the canvas is far from clear as the massive pensive (almost melancholic) man, freely inspired by Michelangelo, peers down at his companion who modestly covers herself. She is a reworking of the temptress in the *Temptation* (Plate 4) with a greater sense of plastic form and stronger lighting that is combined with rich colour in the bright red of the man's costume set off against the blue sky. The rooms of the Consiglio dei Dieci were built under Doge Francesco Donato (1545 to 1553) and the frescoed frieze includes the coat of arms of his successor, Marcantonio Trevisan who died in 1554. The canvases, which must have been begun by 1554, were still under way in 1556 when Sansovino (under the pseudonym Guisconi) referred to the work which was probably finished by 1560 the date of Sansovino's first guide-book to Venice where (for the first time) the decoration is referred to in the past tense.

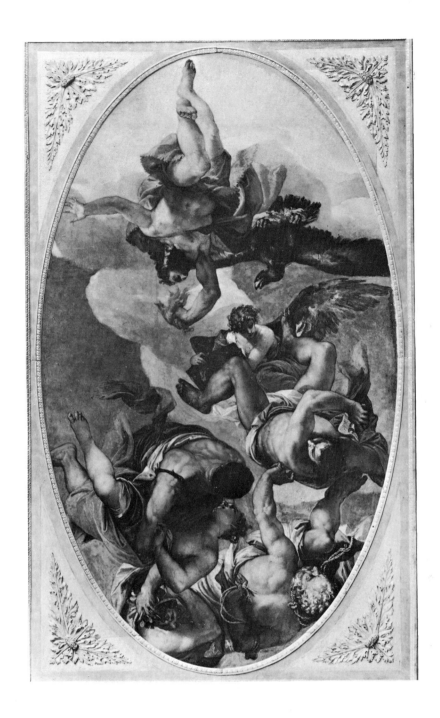

8 Jove Expelling Crimes and Vices

PARIS, Musée du Louvre. 561 × 330 cm.

The canvas originally formed the central oval in the Stanza del Consiglio dei Dieci of the Ducal Palace in Venice, from whence it was taken to Paris in 1797. It was removed to Versailles in 1810 and was later cut to fit the ceiling of Louis XIV's bedroom and was returned to the Louvre in 1858. The foreshortened Jove at the top of the canvas, accompanied by an angel holding the bible, drives out a series of crimes and vices whose wickedness appears to be established in a general rather than a specific sense. Jove's pose derives from that of the Laocoon, which had been used with comparable foreshortening by Tintoretto in his 1548 *Miracle of St. Mark*, Venice, Accademia; the freedom with which the vices are viewed, suggests that they must have been based on small wax models, a practise that Tintoretto also introduced in the 1548 *Miracle* but the inspiration for figures in this degree of movement above the spectator's head comes from the second half of the Sistine ceiling. The programme for this suite of rooms was drawn up by Daniele Barbaro and the present canvas appears to relate to the functions of the Council which had been established after the Tiepolo–Querini plot in 1310 to guard the state against the threat of conspiracy and became responsible for the good conduct of the patricians, and supervised the police, clothes, prostitution etc.

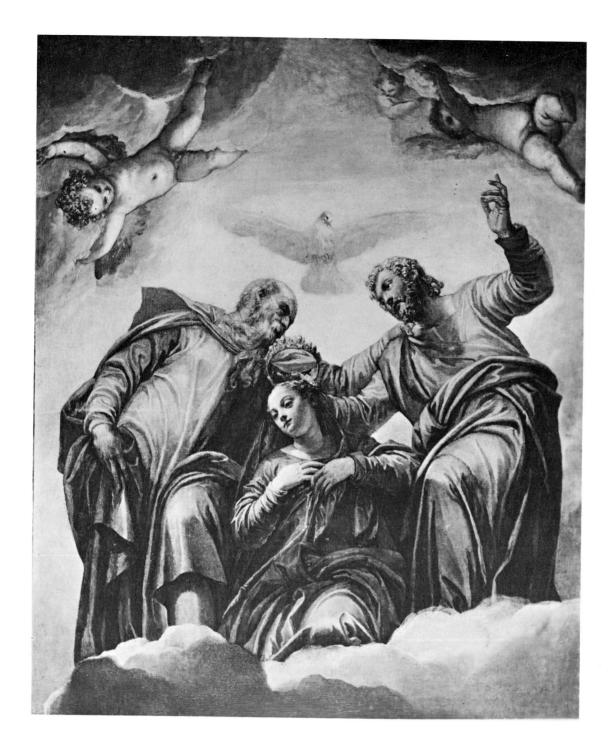

9 Coronation of the Virgin

VENICE, S. Sebastiano, Sacristy. 200 × 170 cm.

The motif of the Virgin kneeling while Christ stands may reflect Tullio Lombardo's marble-relief of this subject in S. Giovanni Crisostomo, although Veronese has linked his figures with an assurance that reflects his study of Raphael. The Sacristy had been built in 1543 and the frame reflects the division of the compartments of Giulio Romano's Sala di Psiche in the Palazzo del Te. That the ceiling was Veronese's first contribution for his fellow Veronese prior, Fra Bernardo Torlione, is confirmed by the tondo held by one of the pairs of cherubim: 'M.D.L.V. DIE XXIII NOVEMBER.' The remaining three pairs hold two inscriptions: 'CORONAM IN CAPITE TUO ACCIPE' and 'ACCIPE DIGNITATEM ET CORONA AETERNAM'. The decoration was completed by the four evangelists (see fig. 4) who witness the Coronation and by a series of strapwork frames with small scenes from the old testament, which reveal his interest in the contemporary work of the sculptor Alessandro Vittoria. The four tondi with cherubim are the work of assistants; the scheme is discussed by Kahr, J.W.C.I., 1970, 235 ff.

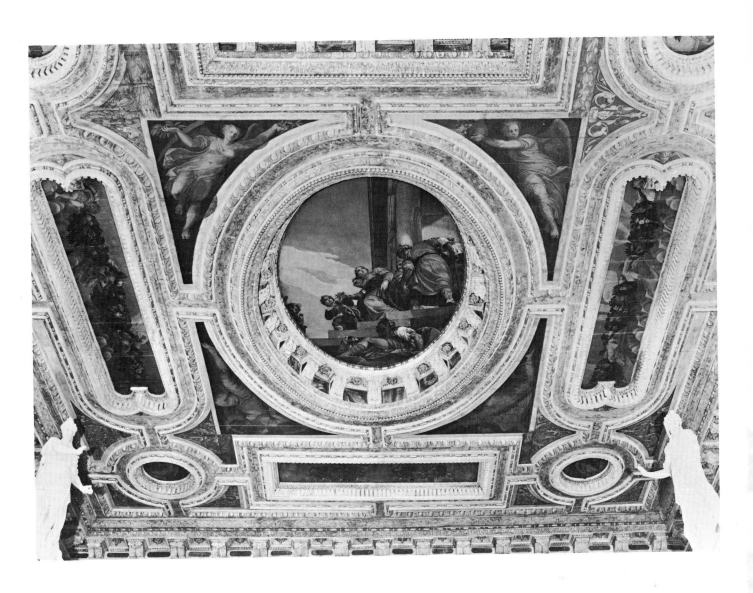

10 Esther Brought before Ahasuerus

VENICE, S. Sebastiano, Nave. 500 × 370 cm.

The title has been questioned by Kahr (J.W.C.I. 1970 235 ff.) who identified the scene as the: *Banishment of Vashti*. We have retained the traditional title partially because Ridolfi (writing in 1648) was generally reliable and because the action with the pathetic figure isolated by her red and green cloak against the yellow of the massive soldier who holds the crown and guards the king on the right of the canvas fits with the frightened Esther being brought to the harem for the first time. In feature she is identical with the Esther of the *Coronation* (Plate 11). The decoration is completed by six balustrades with putti, four roundels with *Hope, Faith, Charity* and *Justice*, two balustrades with masks and eight angels flanking the two oval canvases.

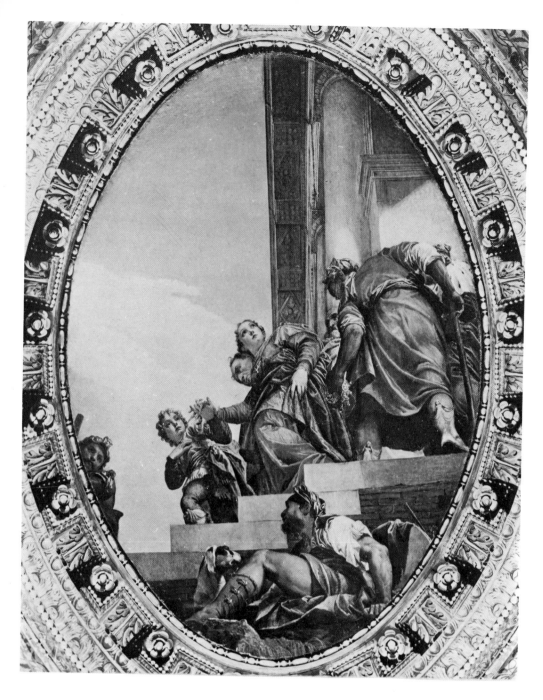

10a　Esther Brought before Ahasuerus

I　Triumph of Mordechai

VENICE, S. Sebastiano, Nave. 500 × 370 cm.

Why were scenes from the Book of Esther chosen for the decoration of the nave of S. Sebastiano? It had not engaged the attention of the early church fathers but the first commentary—that of Rabanus Maurus in the ninth century—established an interpretation of Esther as the church triumphant that is relevant to S. Sebastiano. The flag of the empire waved so prominently in the *Triumph* must allude to the emperor's struggle with protestantism and is to be understood as indicating the triumph of the Catholic cause. It has been suggested that by analogy with the late medieval *Biblia Pauperum* Esther represents the Virgin; the central scene which influenced this doctrine was that of Esther's intercession with Ahasuerus to save the Jews, when she appeared before him unbidden and he put out his sceptre to indicate that Esther was outside the law. The absence of this scene and of that gesture in the *Coronation* suggest that we must see it as an optimistic response to the crises that the Catholic Church had faced since the challenge of Luther in the early decades of the century. A preparatory drawing for the *Triumph* is discussed in B.M., 1972, 322 ff.

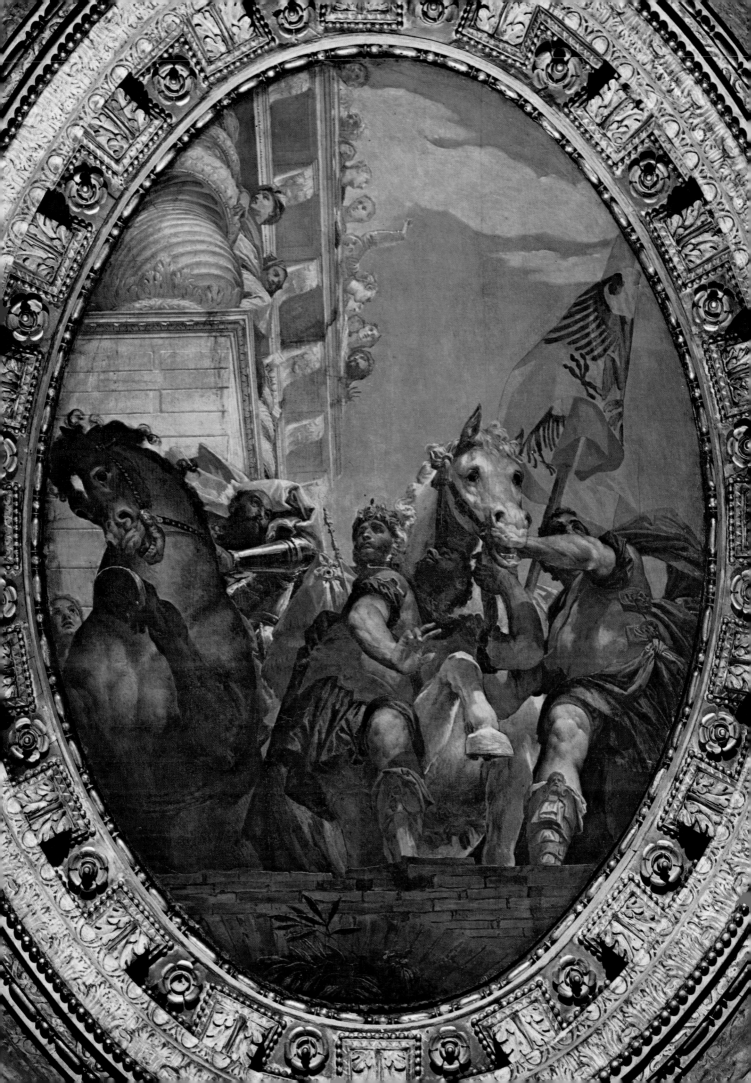

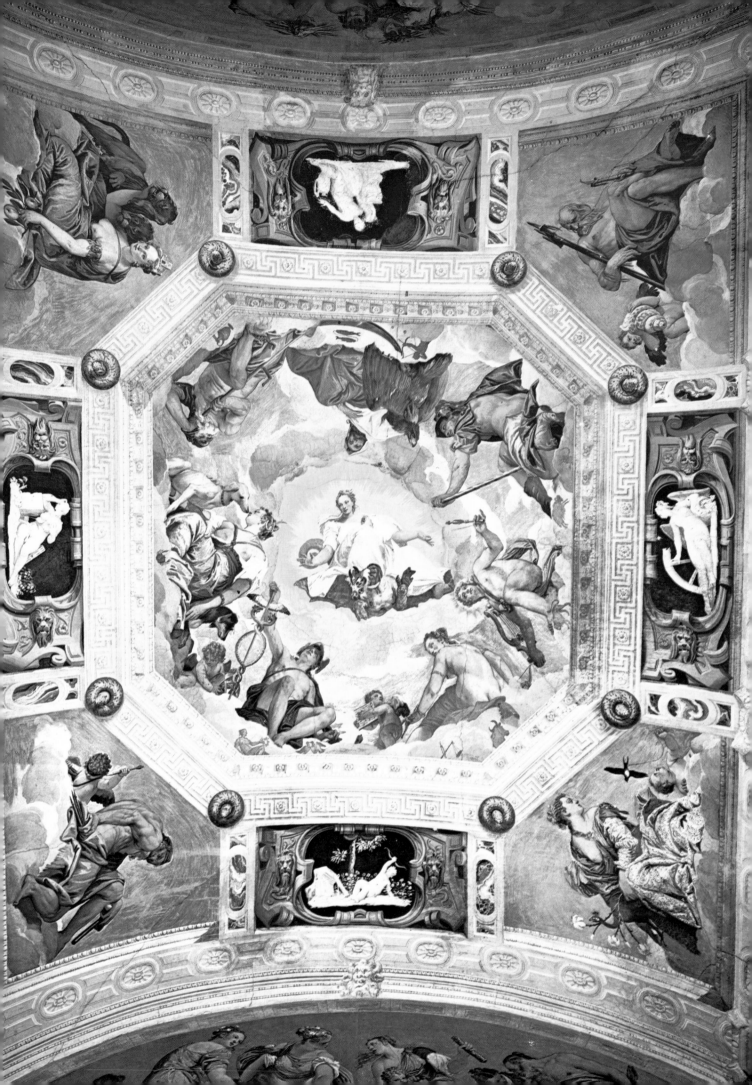

II Ceiling of the Sala Dell'Olympo

MASER, Villa Barbaro (now Volpi) Fresco.

In the outer fields the four elements are symbolized by Vulcan for fire, Cybele for earth, Neptune for water and Juno for Air. In the centre the planets are linked with the zodiacal signs: Saturn with Aquarius and Capricornus, Jupiter with Sagittarius and Pisces, Mars with Aries and Scorpio, Apollo is close to Aries and linked with Leo, Venus with Taurus and Libra, Mercury with Virgo and Gemini and finally Luna with Cancer. The lady riding the huge headless snake has been identified as both Eternity and Truth but she is more likely to be Thalia who would link with the remaining figures and with those of the crossing (Plate 17) in a representation of the harmony of the spheres that fits with Daniele Barbaro's demand for an overall 'effetto'. In the lunette Venus reclines in the lap of her husband Vulcan in reference to Marcantonio's marriage in 1534; the feigned cameo above shows Cupid's triumph in reference to: '*Amor Vincit Omnia*'. The cameo opposite, above the lunette of Bacchus, shows Abundance with a cornucopia and a jug of wine. The two remaining cameos show Fertile Nature and Fortune balancing the good with the bad.

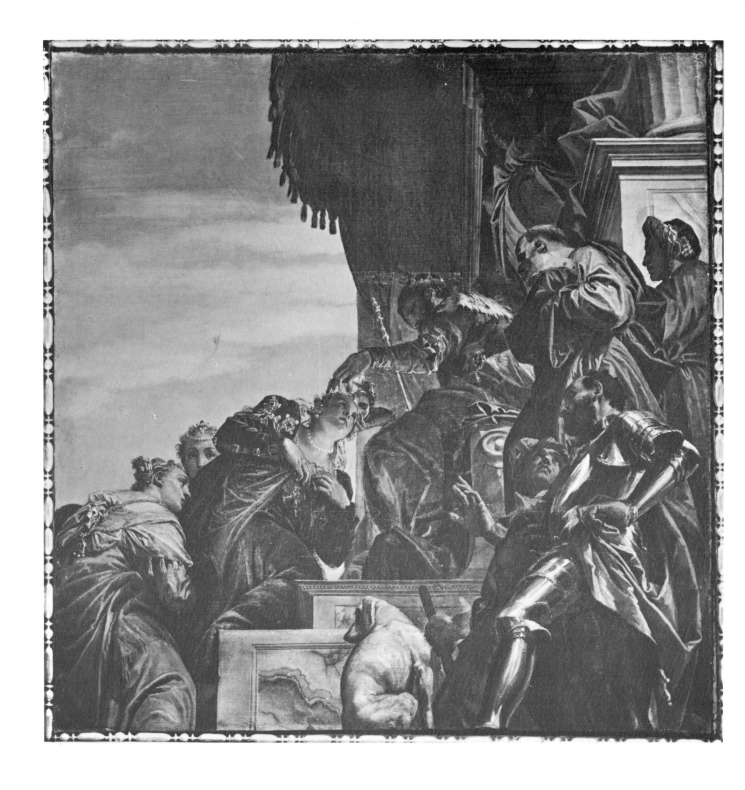

11 Coronation of Esther

VENICE, S. Sebastiano, Nave. 450 × 370 cm.

The *Coronation* had enjoyed a vogue in cassone panels and the composition of this conforms to that tradition, although the connection could be accidental since the pyramidal grouping continues that of Titian's Pesaro altar. Veronese signed the contract for the ceiling paintings on 1 December 1555 and received the final payment on 30 October 1556. There are payments to two assistants but in contrast with the sacristy (Plate 9) all that we see appears to be autograph (although the assistants must have helped with the preparation of the canvases and the lay-in of the figures).

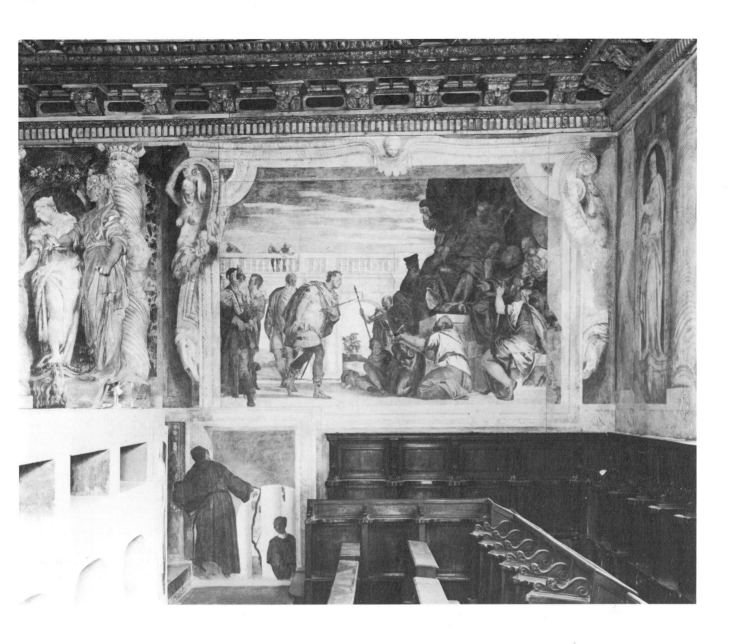

12 St. Sebastian before Diocletian

VENICE, S. Sebastiano, Fresco in the upper part of the Nave. Approx. 330 cm. in height.

The lighting of this fresco which is taken from the window to the spectator's right emphasizes the saint by placing the emperor and his retinue in shadow. Because of damage Veronese covered the fresco with a canvas (the date is uncertain) and it was uncovered in 1762. The canvas has survived only in fragments but its design was recorded in an engraving by N. Cochin. Veronese received 105 ducats for these frescoes on 31 March 1558 and a final 5 ducats on 8 September 1558; the bulk of the work may have been finished by March 1558, and because of the difficulty of working in the winter months, had possibly been carried out in 1557. The ornamentation of the frames reflect the influence of the school of Fontainebleau, the columns link with the work of the Rosa brothers (for whom see Schulz, B.M. 1961, 90 ff.) and the illusionistic doorway is a playful reworking of a device that Pellegrino Tibaldi had contributed to Perino del Vaga's frescoes in the Castel Sant' Angelo, Rome in the late 1540s.

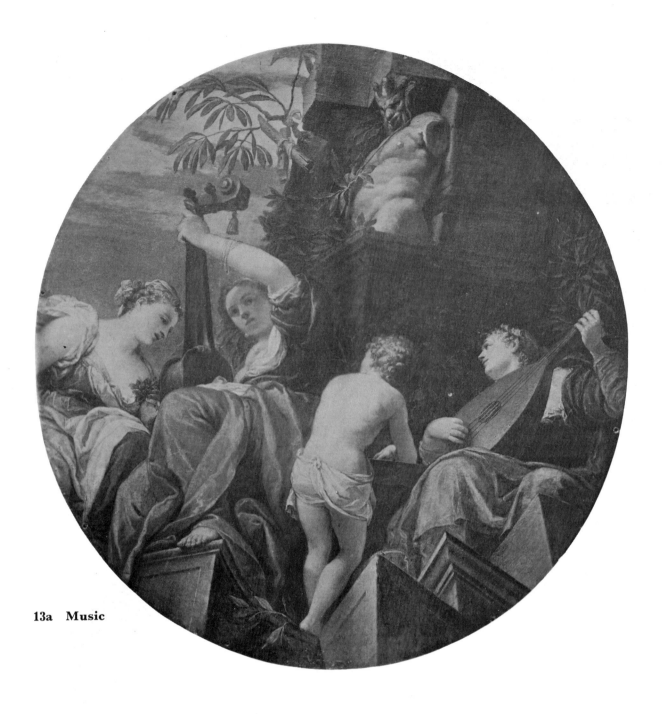

13a Music

13 Music: Arithmetic Music and Philosophy: Honour

VENICE, Libreria Vecchia. Each 230 cm in diameter.

Veronese contributed these three tondi to the ceiling of Sansovino's newly built library between
August 1556 and February 1557; the other artists included Giovanni del Mio, Battista Franco,
Giulio Licinio, Giuseppe Salviati, Andrea Schiavone and Battista Zelotti. Vasari in his enthusiastic
account of *Music* noted that the presence of the wingless Cupid playing the cembalo suggested the
connection of music with love, which is underlined by the flutes hanging near to Pan. The central
tondo shows the connection between music (the woman kneeling with her back to the spectator
holding a flute and just turning from her music) arithmetic (her companion holding a ledger book)
and philosophy embodied in the man who appears to be about to pay tribute to the ruler in the
final tondo which is now difficult to see because the east windows, which lit it, were walled up by
Scamozzi in 1586. The seated ruler, whose throne is supported by Fame, is offered a sacrifice in the
centre of the canvas, the homage of the woman and child, of the servant with the urn and laurel
and of the wise men who bear him a cap. According to the early sources his fellow artists chose
Music as the best canvas in the series for which he was awarded a gold chain by the procurators.

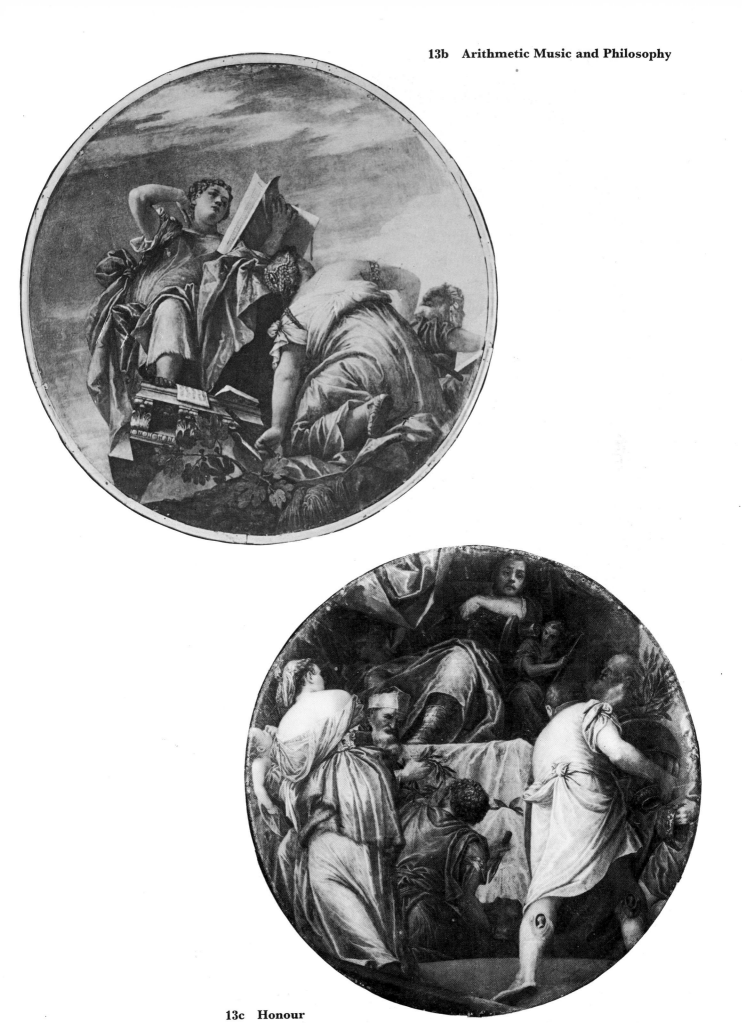

13c Honour

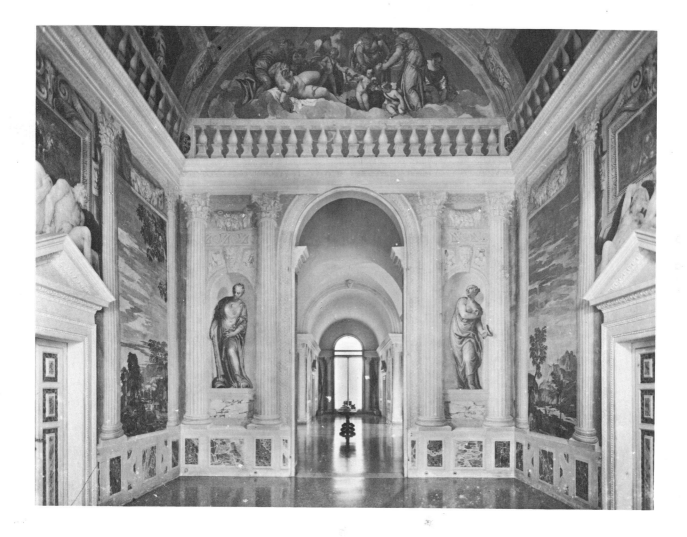

14 Walls of the Sala Dell'Olympo

MASER, Villa Barbaro (now Volpi), Fresco.

The elegant Corinthian columns frame the figures of Peace (on the left) and Faith (on the right); the grisaille frescoes above the two doors at the side embody the best principles of Antiquity and Christianity in *Marcus Curtius* and the *Good Samaritan*. Above the balustrade on the left two boys are shown holding a dog and a book while on the right a nurse, a mother and a young child look in. This view shows the room as it appears to the spectator who has just left the nymphaeum and looks towards the crossing (Plate 17). A letter written to Daniele Barbaro in 1559 refers to the nymphaeum, which shows that Vittoria must have worked at the villa by 1559, and it seems possible that this provides the date for Veronese's work in the villa (see for this and the detailed account of the decoration, J.W.C.I. 1972, 226 ff.).

15 Ceiling, Stanza del Cane

MASER, Villa Barbaro (now Volpi), Fresco.

Discord, identified by her knife, sits to the left threatening the back of the standing lady who is squabbling with the lady seated on the globe for the cornucopia. The lion at the feet of the central figure identifies her as Munificence while the globe and the cornocopia are the attributes of Providence. The general message of this room (to the west of the Sala dell'Olympo), which is echoed in the room on the other side where it is put in Christian terms, is: Charity must be tempered by Foresight lest it give rise to Discord. This fits with the Aristotelian temper of Daniele Barbaro's introduction to his edition of Vitruvius where he expressed the view that: 'Prudence is the mode which makes the intellect regulate the will in those things which contribute to one's own good, it is that which makes us just, modest etc.' The fresco beneath is probably a warning not to be lulled by fickle fortune while that on the other side with Saturn and a companion who is either Meditation or History is less easy to interpret.

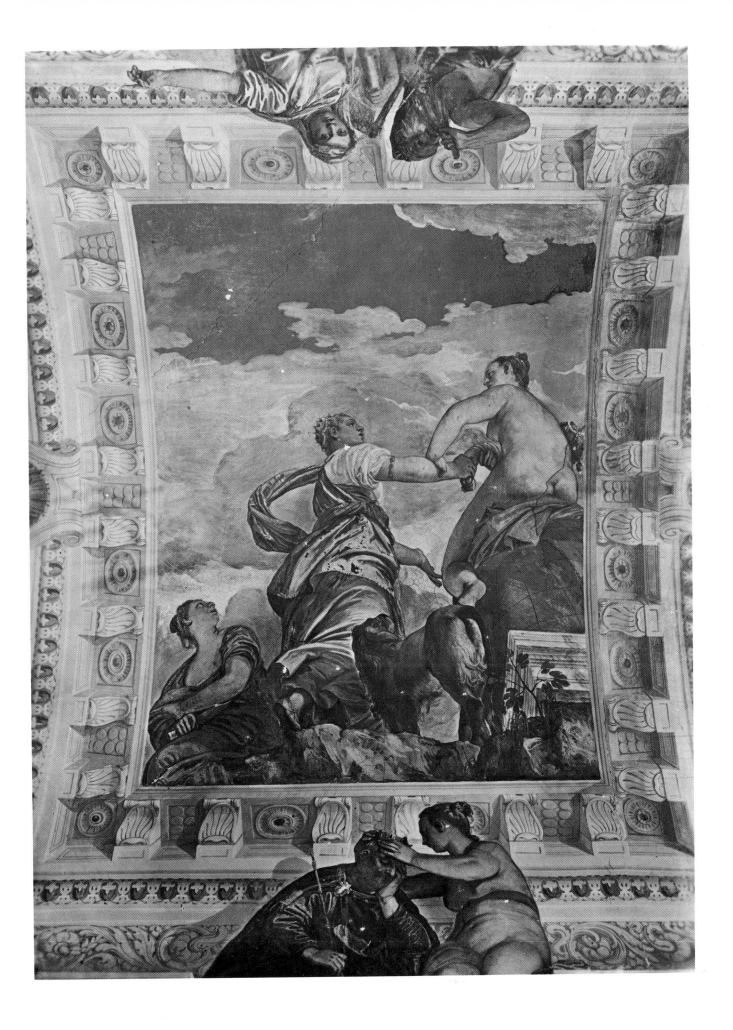

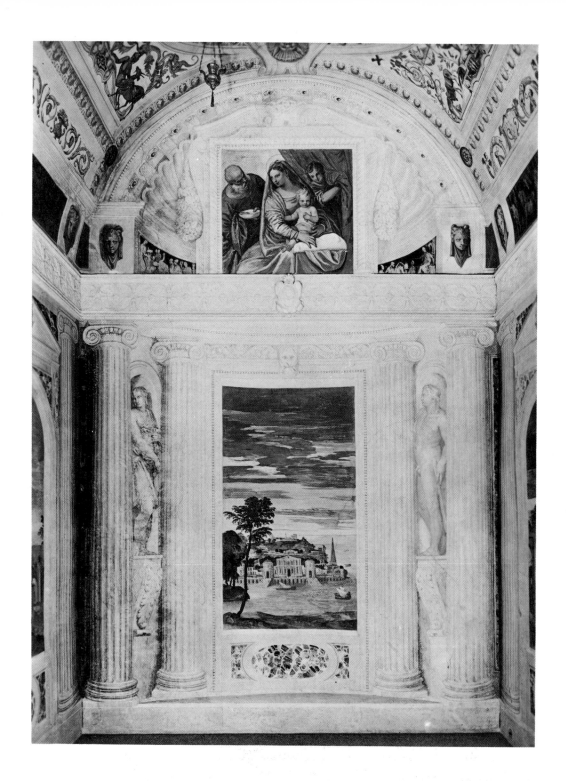

16   Walls of the Stanza della Lucerna

MASER, Villa Barbaro (Now Volpi), Fresco.

Both here and in Plate 15 the walls are dominated by the appearance of the Holy Family in a (painted) frame above the cornice. This is taken up in the ceiling fresco with its emphasis upon the primacy of the Catholic Faith which had a special relevance for Daniele Barbaro who as Patriarch Elect of Aquileia had played an important part in refuting the charges of heresy faced by the Patriarch, Giovanni Grimani, at the Council of Trent in 1562. The Ionic columns differentiate this room and the Stanza del Cane from the Sala dell'Olympo and the Crossing, which are linked thematically. The brilliant evocation of a classical sea-port was achieved with the inspiration of literary rather than visual models*.

> * For a rather different view of these landscapes see A. R. Turner, *The Vision of Landscape in Renaissance Italy*, Princeton 1966.

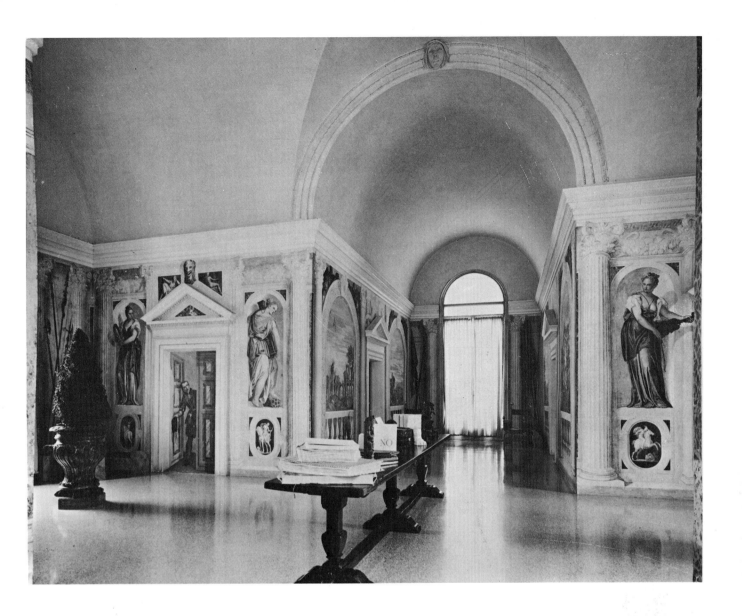

17 Walls of the Crossing

MASER, Villa Barbaro (Now Volpi), Fresco.

This view continues that of the walls of the Sala dell'Olympo looking to the window on
the main south facade. We see three of the eight musical ladies who inhabit the niches of the
crossing while the remainder of the walls are frescoed with landscapes set behind balustrades. The
boy entering through the fictive door balances a real door opposite and the illusion, which was
first used at S. Sebastiano, was used again on the balancing wall to the right and again in one of
the rooms after the Stanza della Lucerna, where a hunter is shown entering the villa. The eight
ladies in the crossing were identified as Muses by early sources and this can be sustained if we
assume that the ninth (Thalia) is in the centre of the ceiling of the Sala dell'Olympo (Plate II);
the view that the programme illustrated the harmony of the spheres would explain the emphasis
upon musical instruments in this fresco. The walls have suffered terribly at the hands of the
Austrians in the nineteenth century who slashed many of the landscapes; there was formerly a
trellis on the ceiling of this room.

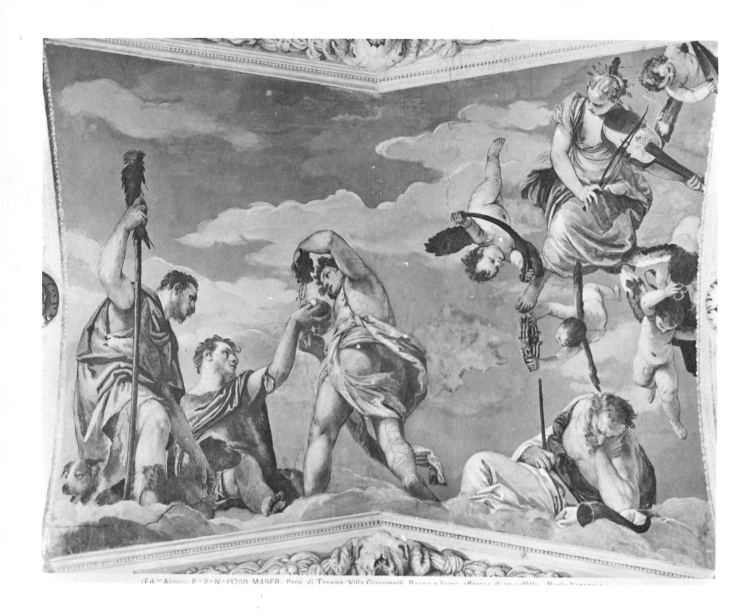

18 Ceiling of the Stanza di Bacco

MASER, Villa Barbaro (Now Volpi). Fresco.

The central opening is completed by the trellis that can be seen in Plate 19. Bacchus pressing grapes into the cup held up by the huntsman appears as a god of fertility both here and in one of the lunettes in the Sala dell'Olympo where he is accompanied by Abundance and Ceres, who in this room is seated above the fireplace with Pluto. The Barbaros had owned a farm at Maser at least since 1514 and it had been enlarged before the commission to Palladio to rebuild the villa and its farm buildings sometime in the 1550s. The invocation of Bacchus as a god of fertility is a suitable choice of subject for a villa that was used as a farm, but here it is linked with his other role, as leader of the Muses, whose music is heard on the right of the fresco. In the companion room at the front of the house Venus is linked with Mars, in celebration of marriage.

42

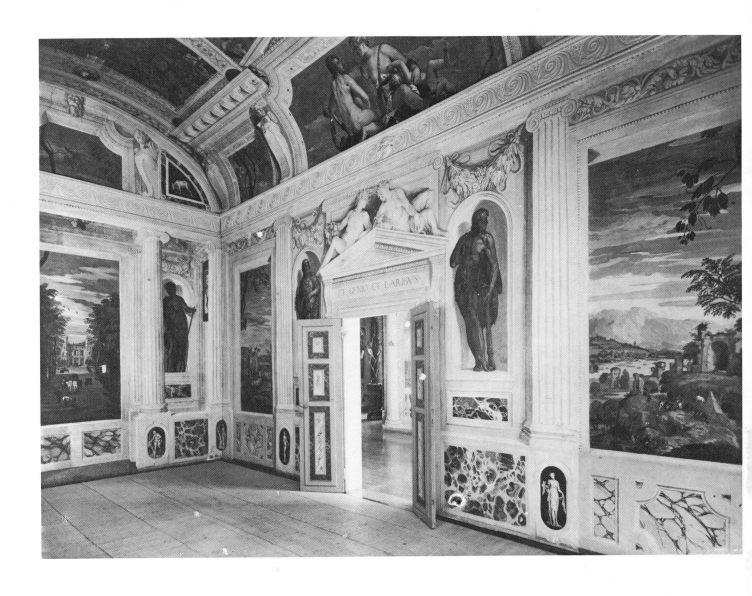

19 Walls of the Stanza di Bacco

MASER, Villa Barbaro (Now Volpi). Fresco.

Apollo with his lyre and Venus about to give suck to Cupid echo the dual role of Bacchus as god
of fertility and of music in the centre of the ceiling. Both the depth of the illusionistic walls and the
brilliance of the colour reveal the invention with which Veronese transforms traditional schemes.
The fireplace (opposite the doorway) established a rhythm for the Ionic pilasters of the walls
which is taken up by the squat caryatids above the cornice, which echo those designed by
Sebastiano Serlio. The vine spreads over the trellis and down over part of the landscapes; this
illustration of the *locus amoenus*, which derives from the upper logge in the Vatican decorated by the
Raphael workshop, is inspired by part of Pliny the younger's description of his Tuscan villa:
'Another room is situated close to the nearest plane tree, its sides are covered with marble up to
the cornice; on a frieze above the foliage is painted with birds perched among the branches; in this
room is placed a little fountain.'

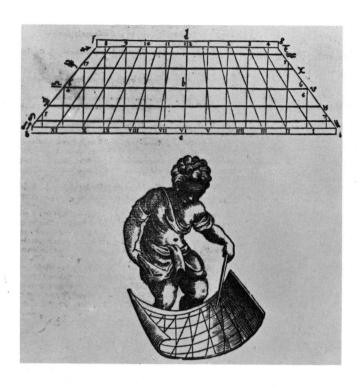

20a   Detail of illustration from 1556 edition of Vitruvius

20   Portrait of Daniele Barbaro

AMSTERDAM, Rijksmuseum. 118 × 104 cm.

The picture was first recorded in the Hensler collection, Bâle, in 1726 from whom it was acquired by Otto Lanz, Amsterdam by 1929 whence it passed to the museum in 1952. The sitter's identity is established by the 1556 edition of Vitruvius at which he his looking. The comparative illustration of page 235, Plate 20a, shows how Veronese has reworked the illustration which he has combined with a temple facade taken from Book Three; this illustration does not recur in Book Nine of the 1567 edition where the frontispiece has also been changed. These changes, together with the contact between Veronese and Barbaro in the mid 1550s (see Plates 8 and II) suggest a date of around 1556 for the portrait. He appears as a younger man, not in ecclesiastical garb (he became Patriarch elect of Aquileia in 1550) in the 1545 portrait by Titian which is now in National Gallery of Canada. A smaller portrait of a Patriarch of Aquileia (presumably but not necessarily Barbaro) was no. 65 in the 1682 inventory of Veronese's heirs with dimensions of about 51 × 42 cm. It might be the version in the Foscarini collection, which was engraved by Cattini (d. 1800). It is clear from other examples that Veronese made small portraits from life, which he then re-used in larger portraits. Another version, now lost, of the Amsterdam portrait was sold from Consul Smith's collection in 1762.

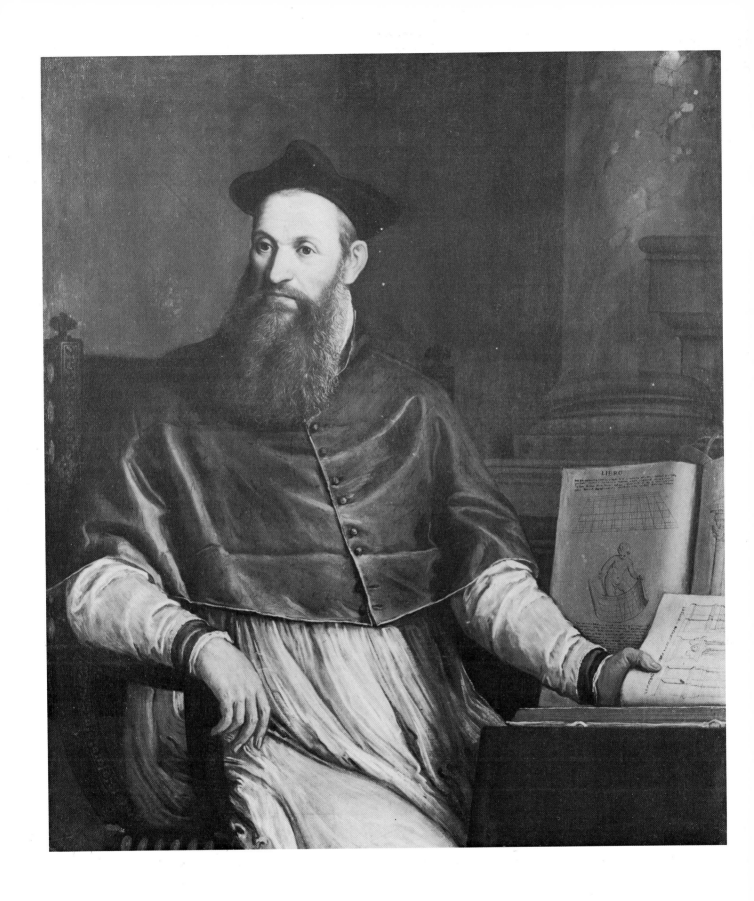

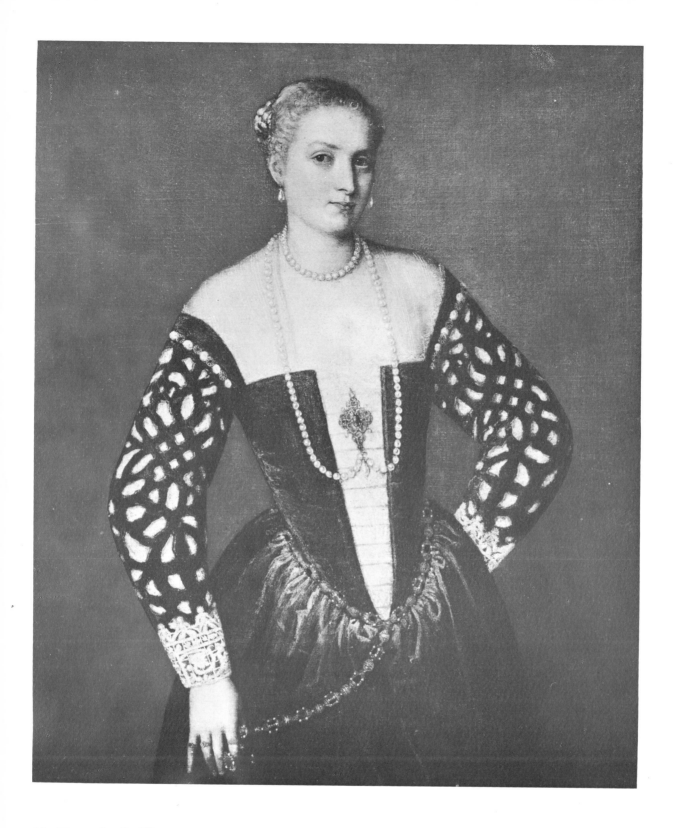

21 Portrait of a Woman

DOUAI, Musée des Beaux-Arts. 106 × 87 cm.

This splendid portrait was bought from the collection of the Duc de Luynes by Mme. Wagner who sold it to the Museum in 1871. The directness with which the sitter is presented is matched by the *Belle Nani* in the Louvre and by the seated portrait of a woman with a small dog in Madrid. This is modified in the portrait in Lugano by the introduction of a curtain and the prominence given to the dog; the curtain recurs in the portrait in Munich and in the portrait of a woman in Vienna who caresses a swan. This idea is carried one stage further in a picture in Hamble, Hampshire, where the rich brocade thrown over the sitter, the prayer book and the lamb suggest that she is posing as St. Agnes, in anticipation of her forthcoming marriage, a device that Van Dyck used in his portraits of the 1630s.

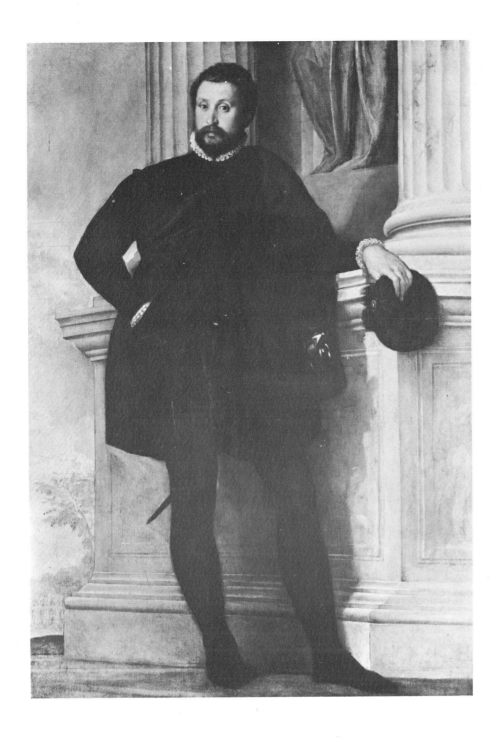

22 Portrait of a Man

MALIBU, Getty Collection. 193 × 135 cm.

This picture which was acquired for its present collection from Wildenstein in 1955, is not recorded in any sources before its sale by the Countess Salvi Pindemonte-Moscardo to Richard Pryor in 1802. At that time it was engraved as a self-portrait, but comparison with the self-portrait in the *Marriage Feast* (Plate IIIa) shows that this late tradition is unreliable; the view of St. Mark's in the background suggests that the sitter may be a procurator. The ease with which the figure stands in front of the architecture develops from the 1551 Francheschini portrait in Sarasota and the *Portrait of Giuseppe da Porto with his son Adriano* in the Contini-Bonacossi Bequest, Florence which is usually dated to around 1556 on the evidence of the age of the children who accompany da Porto and his wife in the rubbed companion painting in Baltimore. The figure is related to the colonnade with greater assurance in the three-quarter length *Portrait of Alessandro Contarini* in Dresden which must date to the early 1570s. He reappears (to all appearances unchanged) as an admiral in a portrait in Philadelphia in whose background we see a galley which may be the St. Christopher of which he was in charge in 1570; although wounded he fought in the Battle of Lepanto in 1571, the approximate date of the Dresden and Philadelphia portraits.

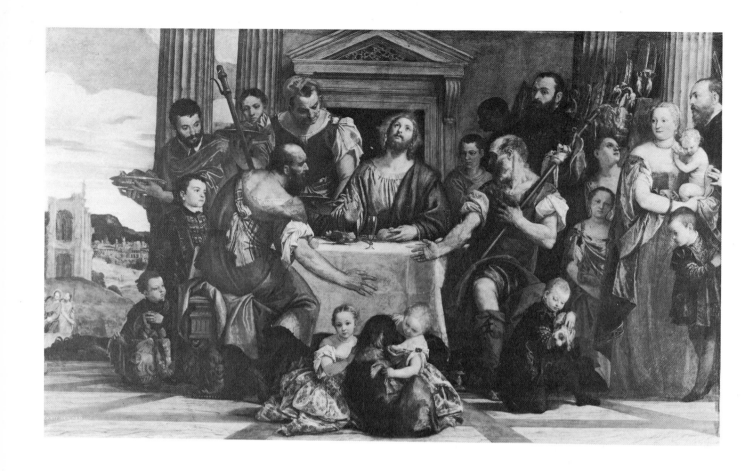

23 Supper at Emmaus

PARIS, Musée du Louvre. 290 × 440 cm.

In the distance we see Christ walking with the two apostles who recognize him as he blesses the bread; the central group was much admired at Le Nôtre's 1667 conférence on the painting where it was rightly argued that the breach of decorum caused by the unidentified donors' enthusiasm to witness the scene was not the responsibility of the artist. We can, however, see the skill with which later Veronese was to cope with a comparable problem in the 1571 *Coccina Family* (Plate 42) where the marble columns divided the earthly sphere from the heavenly. Both because of this and because of the colour the picture has always been dated to the 1550s. It was first recorded in the 1635 inventory of the collection of Charles Emanuel II with a note that it had been given to the Duke of Créqui who was then campaigning for Charles Emanuel in Savoy. Subsequently it was in the collection of Richelieu and although not included in the list of paintings ceded to the King in 1665 was in the Royal Collection by 1667, the date of Le Nôtre's conférence. There are two later autograph versions, from the 1570s, in Dresden and Rotterdam.

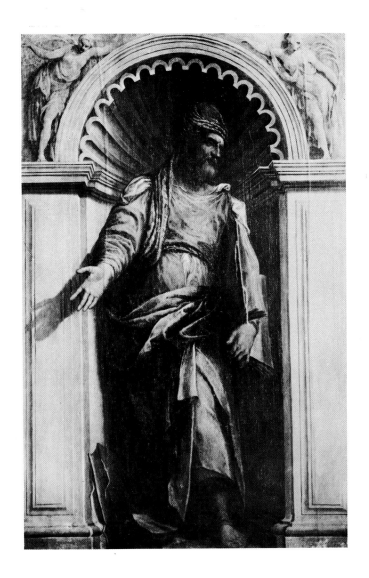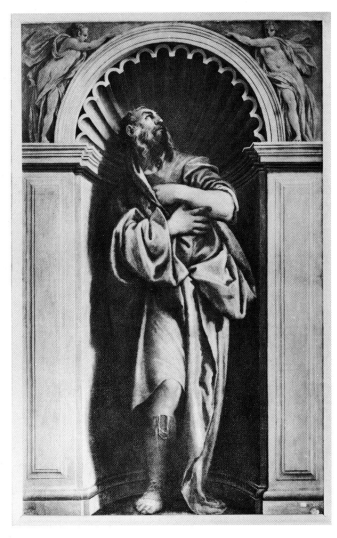

24 Two Philosophers

VENICE, Libreria Vecchia. Each 250 × 160 cm.

These figures, who develop the style of the apostles in the upper part of S. Sebastiano (Plate 12) formed part of a series of twelve painted for the Library in 1560. They have often been moved and were clearly not designed for their present position flanking the entrance door of the main reading room. There were once four philosophers in the vestibule leading to the reading room who were removed in the 1590s when the Grimani collection was placed there; in July 1560 (some months after the payment to Veronese) the vestibule was granted to Federico Badoer's Academy where the Venetian nobility were, for a time at least, taught Greek. The two philosophers by Veronese may well have formed part of this scheme, the one with the book encouraging the young nobles in their study while his companion looked up at Titian's *Allegory of Wisdom* on the ceiling, the source of their learning.

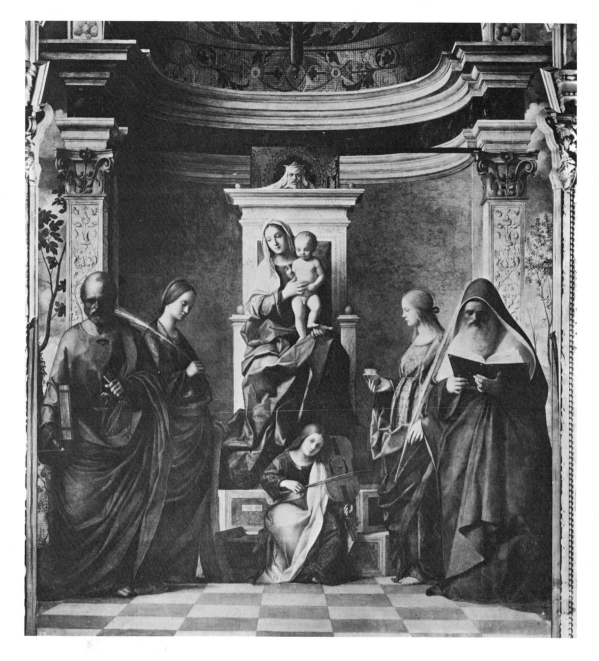

25a GIOVANNI BELLINI
S. Zaccaria altar
VENICE, S. ZACCARIA

25 SS. Geminianus and Severus

MODENA, Galleria Estense. 441 × 240 cm.

The saints formed the outside of the organ shutters from the now destroyed church of S. Geminiano, Venice; on the inside were SS. John the Baptist and Mennas. The saints with their brilliant costumes look towards the main altar of the church and are set in front of a niche that recalls that of Bellini's S. Zaccaria altar (Plate 25a) with a festoon in the upper part that derives from the work of Giovanni da Udine in Rome. The unification of the organ-shutters when closed follows a Venetian tradition that had begun with Giovanni Bellini and continued with Sebastiano del Piombo. In 1558 Benedetto Manzoni had undertaken to pay for the new organ which is referred to as finished by Sansovino in 1561 who also explicitly mentions the paintings. The engraving from Plate 52 of Coronelli's, *Singolarità di Venezia* (ca. 1709) (Plate 25b) shows the old, round-headed, organ that was replaced by a square one in the early years of the eighteenth century (it is shown on Plate 50 of Coronelli); the present canvases have been adjusted to fit with the new organ while the other two saints were cut down. They were removed at the time of the destruction of the church in 1807 and were reunited in Modena in 1924.

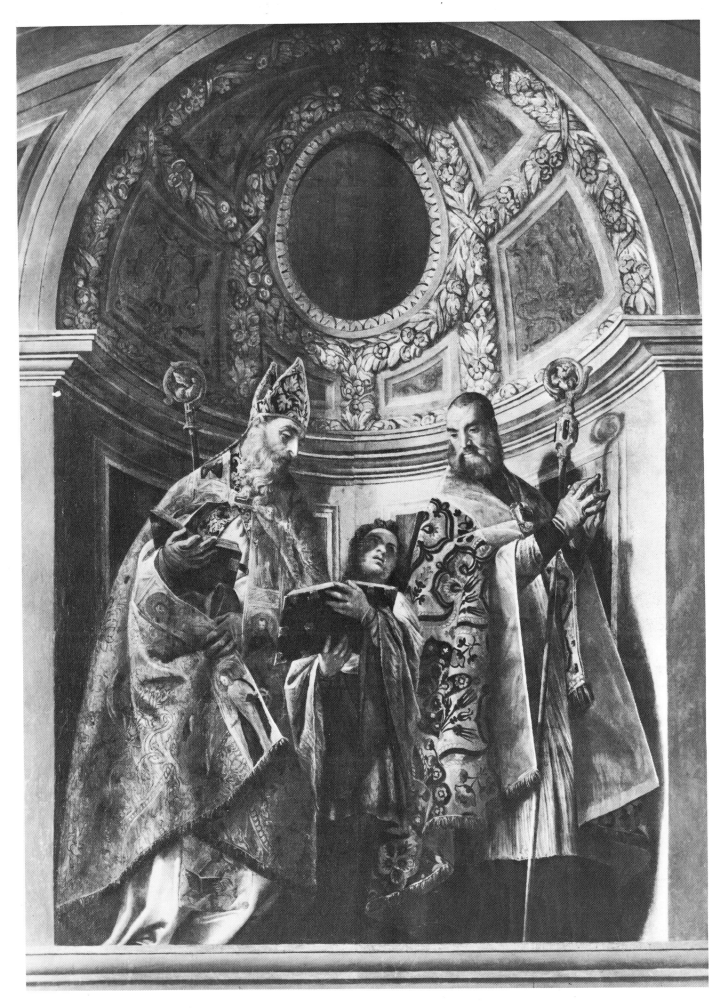

51

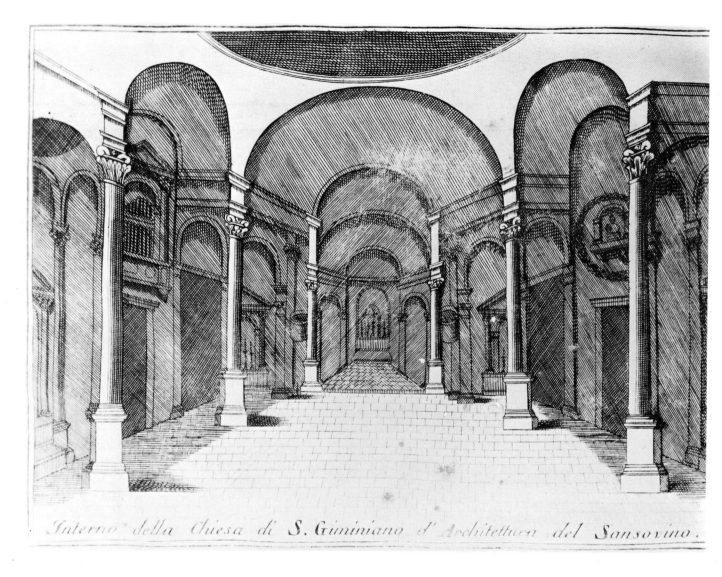

Interno della Chiesa di S. Giminiano d'Architettura del Sansovino.

**25b   View of the interior of S. Geminiano, Venice,
from V. Coronelli**
Singolarità di Venezia; Venice (c. 1709)

26   Presentation of Christ

VENICE, S. Sebastiano, Organ. 490 × 185 cm.

The organ, which covers some of the frescoes in the upper nave of the church, was built by
Domenico Marangone to the design of Veronese beginning in October 1558 and Veronese received
the final payment for his canvases in April 1560. Few earlier Italian organs have survived, but a
comparison with those and with earlier Venetian altars suggests that Veronese's simple and effective
design with the arch breaking through the pediment was an innovation, which may derive from the
illustration of an antique doorway outside Rome by Sebastiano Serlio. The *Presentation* reworks the
version in Dresden with greater clarity: the fussy detail of the Dresden canvas has gone, the altar
for instance, is covered by a drape, both the page holding the bowl in the foreground and the lady
with the basket of doves (a traditional element in the ceremony of the Purification, as are the
candles held by St. Joseph) look at the central group.

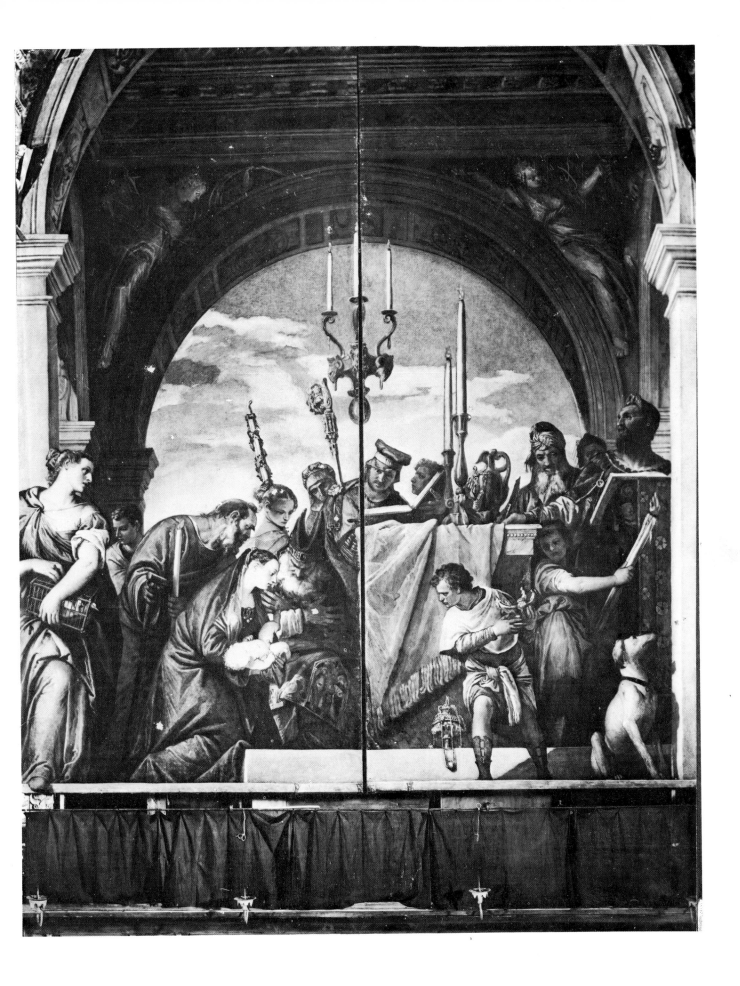

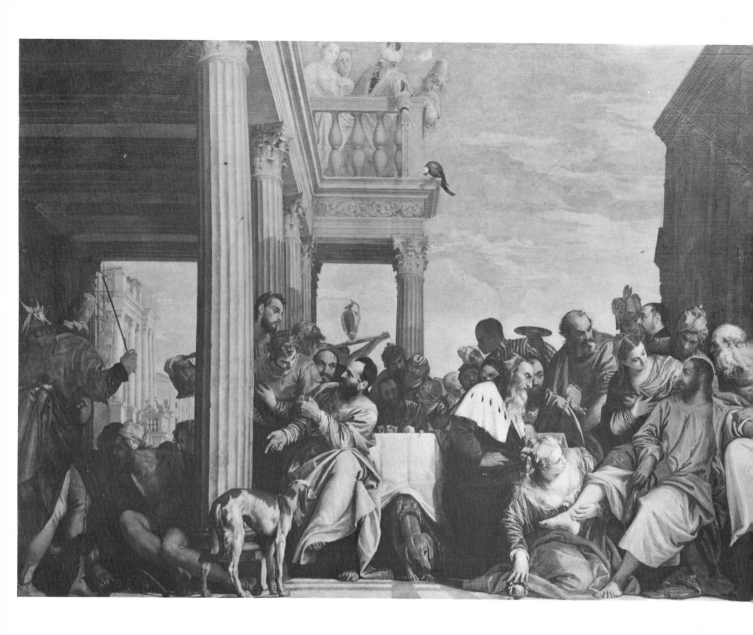

27 Feast in the House of Simon

TURIN, Galleria Sabauda. 315 × 451 cm.

Both in colour and in the architecture the picture, whose date is always taken to be ca. 1560, fits with the organ shutters of S. Sebastiano (Plate 26) which are documented as being finished in that year. The red of Christ's robe, which is the lightest tone in the canvas, offsets the shadow in which he is placed, and is the focal point of the colour, while the Magdalen at his feet is bathed in light as she gazes at him. The *Feast* had traditionally formed a part of cycles of Mary Magdalen and only in the sixteenth century did it become an isolated subject painted in a refectory. Moretto's version of 1544 painted for SS. Fermo e Rustico, Monselice, stayed close to Marcantonio's engraving of this subject, adding a few servants at the sides. Veronese who filled his canvas with more detail looked back to Carpaccio and possibly to Mantegna for the low view-point and the opening in the relief-like grouping in the centre, which recalls the frescoes in the Eremitani. The picture, which was painted for the refectory of SS. Nazaro e Celso, Verona was acquired by the Spinola, Genoa in 1650 from whom it passed to Carlo Alberto in 1825 and thence to the gallery in 1832.

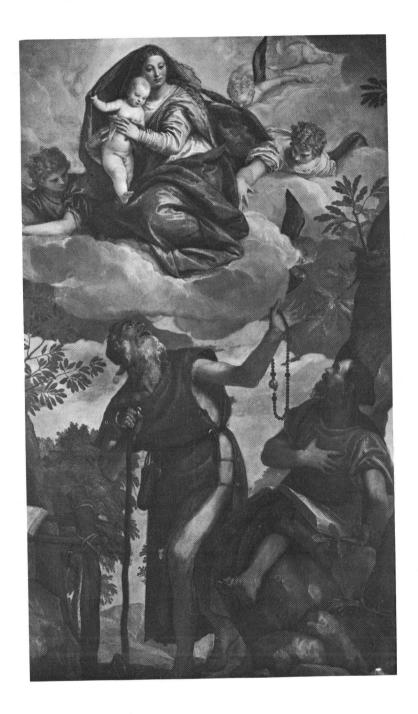

28   Virgin and Child Appear to SS. Anthony and Paul

NORFOLK, Va. Walter P. Chrysler Museum, 285 × 170 cm.

The *Virgin and Child* was the second altar on the right and the *Consecration* the third in the church of S. Benedetto Po; Veronese received the commission in December 1561 and had completed it by March 1562. His *St. Jerome* from the first chapel on the right was, like the *Consecration*, sold to England but destroyed by fire in 1836; the copy in the church shows that, like the two surviving canvases, it emphasized the appearance of the Virgin to the saint in the desert. The earlier fresco of St. Anthony Abbot in the lunette above the second chapel, which shows him eating in the rocky desert, contrasts with the emphasis upon the heavenly intervention in Veronese's canvases; there is no need for an angel to carry down St. Nicholas's mitre and staff and the appearance of the Virgin to both St. Anthony and St. Jerome is unusual. The pictures all remained *in situ* until at least 1763; the copies that replaced them were probably made in the 1790s when the originals were displayed in a gallery in the monastery. The Napoleonic suppression of parish churches led to their removal; the *Consecration* was sold in London in June 1814 when it was bought by the British Institution by which it was presented to the Gallery in 1826. The *Virgin and Child* moved to Mantua and then to a private collection in France from where it passed to the present collection in 1962.

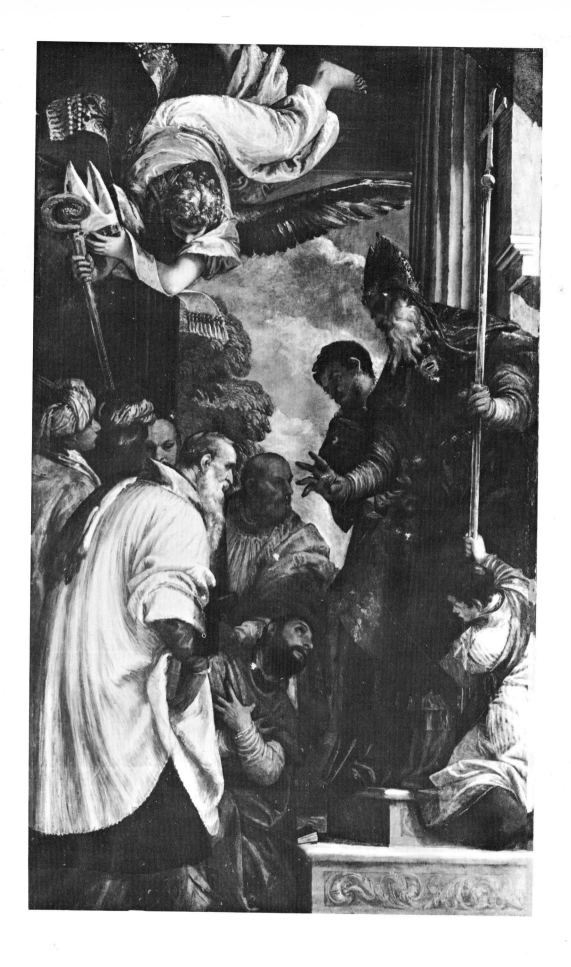

28a   Consecration of St. Nicholas

LONDON, National Gallery. 282 × 170 cm.

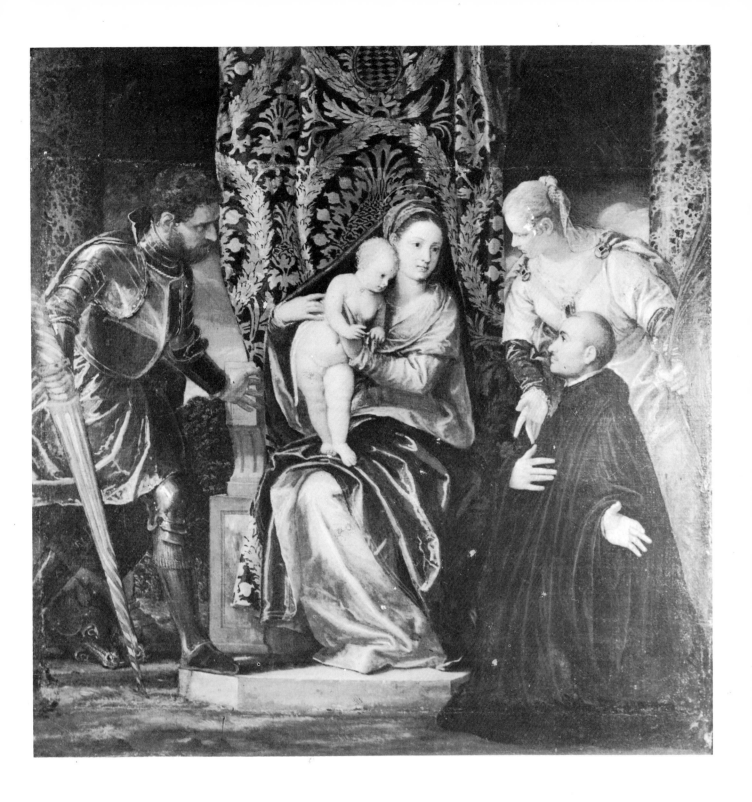

29 Holy Family with SS. George, Justina and a Donor (Girolamo Scrocchetto?)

PARIS, Musée du Louvre. 90 × 90 cm.

The first mention of this painting, in the 1662 catalogue of the de Brienne collection, noted the connection of the saints with S. Giorgio Maggiore. This can be taken one stage further for the donor closely resembles the guest on the right of the *Feast* (Plate 30b) whose costume indicates that he is likely to be Girolamo Scrocchetto, the abbot responsible for the commission. He is smoother-featured and younger in appearance in the present picture, which was presumably painted during 1551–54, the first period during which he was abbot of S. Giorgio. The rich marble of the columns at the side as well as the patterned cloth of honour recall the older Venetian tradition represented by Cima. The picture was in the French Royal collection by 1683.

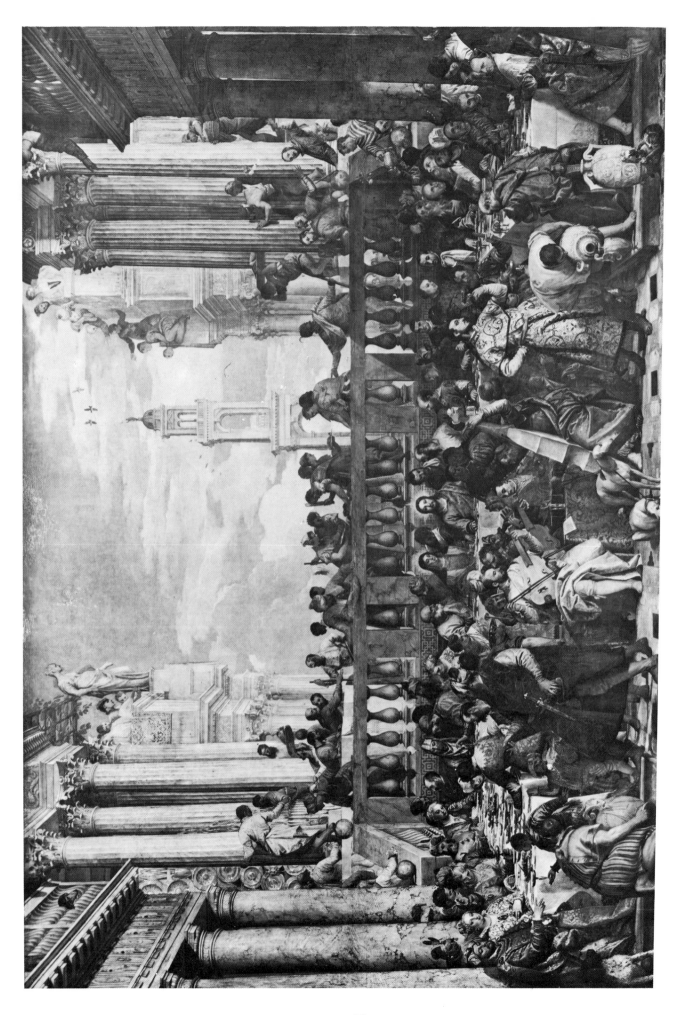

30 Marriage Feast at Cana

PARIS, Musée du Louvre. 669 × 990 cm.

This enormous canvas was painted for the refectory of S. Giorgio Maggiore from June 1562 until September 1563; it was removed to Paris in 1797 and placed in the Louvre in 1801. Writing in 1611 Thomas Coryate noted that the monastery was: 'a passing sumptuous place, and the fairest and richest monastery without comparison in all Venice, having at least three-score crowns for a yearly revenue.' This, as modern scholars have observed, played its part in the *Feast* but as we emphasized in the text it is counteracted by the servants' awareness of the miracle. This reading finds confirmation in the version of this subject that Veronese painted for the Coccina family in ca. 1571, now in Dresden. In the preparatory sketch for the painting, in Berlin, the servant contemplating the glass of wine (the motif found on the right of Plate 30a) is combined with others pouring wine at the foot of the round table. In the painting the motifs are separated, the pouring becomes an incidental detail in the background, while the glass that the servant contemplates is given new significance by being juxtaposed with Christ's head. It is possible that the symmetrical wings, the horizontal division behind Christ, the inclusion of the family's plate and of the musicians may have been suggested by Francesco Salviati's otherwise very different fresco of the *Feast* in S. Salvatore in Lauro, Rome, which may have been finished by 1555.

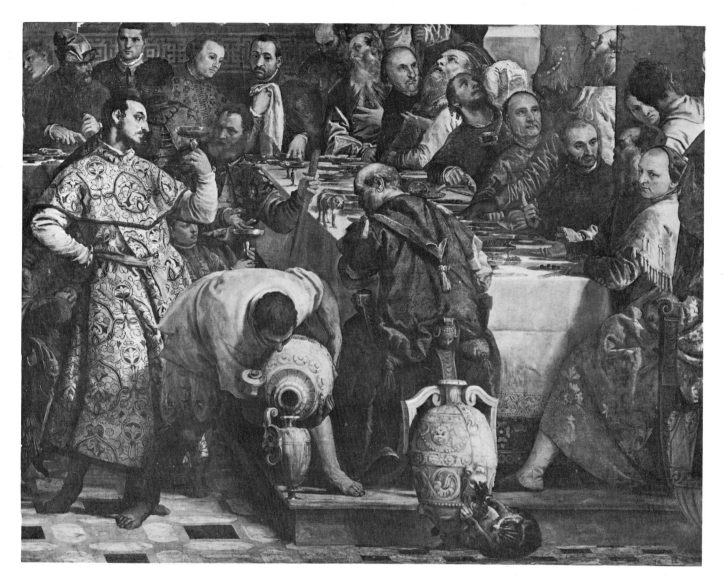

30b   Detail of Plate 30

31   Holy Family with SS. John the Baptist, Francis, Jerome and Justina

VENICE, Gallerie dell'Accademia. 333 × 191 cm.

The altar was painted for the sacristy of S. Zaccaria at the commission of Francesco Bonaldi who in 1562 was given permission to rebuild it in memory of his father, Jerome, and of one of his sons John, both of whom had died the previous year. It was removed to Paris at the orders of Napoleon in 1797 and returned to the Accademia in 1815. The picture must date from the 1560s; the energy with which the saints communicate with the Holy Family is found in the much dirtier Marogna altar in S. Polo, Verona of 1565. Three small devotional canvases link with these two paintings: the *Virgin and Child with Michele Spavento and an Unidentified Saint* in S. Sebastiano, the *Holy Family with St. John the Baptist* in S. Barnaba and the *Virgin and Child with St. Peter and an Unidentified Saint* in the Museo Civico, Vicenza.

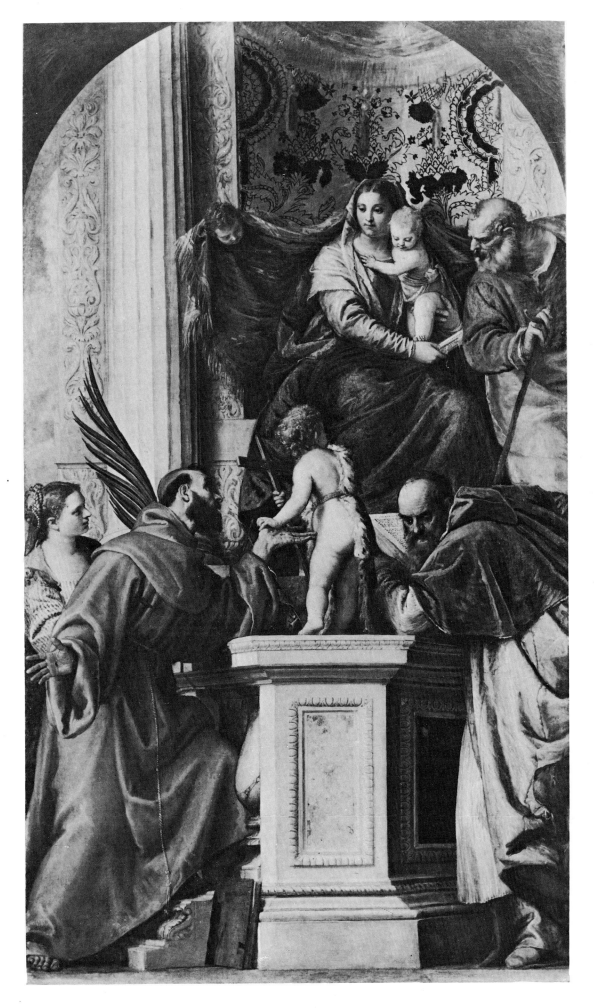

32   Virgin and Child appear to SS. Sebastian, John the Baptist, Peter, Catherine and Elizabeth (?)

VENICE, Sebastiano. 420 × 230 cm.

This is the main altar of S. Sebastiano which had been built by Salvador Tagiapietra between 1559 and 1561 to a design by Veronese. The original commission had been given by Catheruza Cornaro (hence the presence of St. Catherine) in 1546 but it was only built at the orders of her executor Lisa Querini (the St. Elizabeth). Pignatti has suggested that the altar may be slightly later, and comparison with the altars from S. Benedetto Po (Plates 28 and 28a) confirms this; it may have been painted in 1565, at which date Veronese received payment for unspecified work that probably included the lateral canvases (Plates 33 and 34). The altar is flanked by frescoes of *SS. Paul and Honofrius*, and the scheme was originally completed by the *Assumption of the Virgin, God the Father, Angels, Doctors of the Church* and *Evangelists* which were replaced by Sebastiano Ricci in c. 1700 when the cupola threatened to collapse.

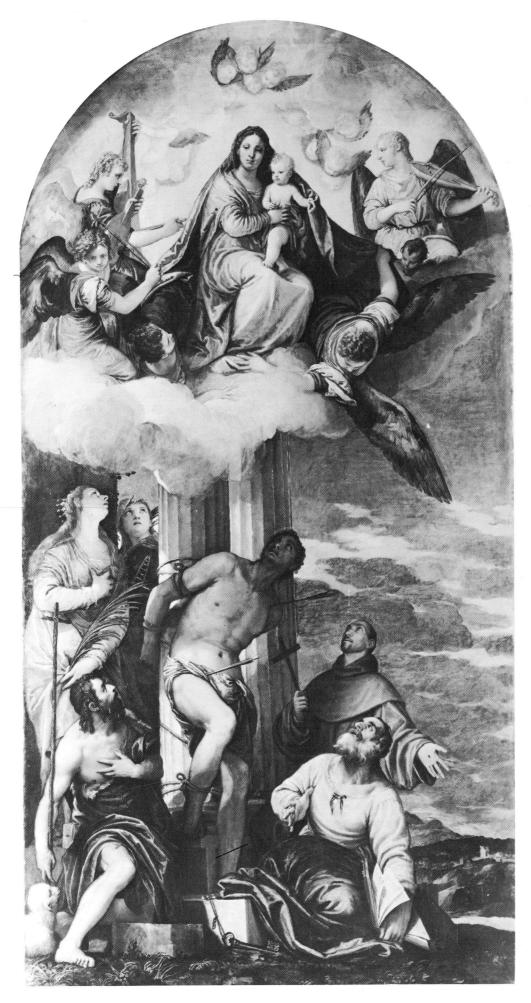

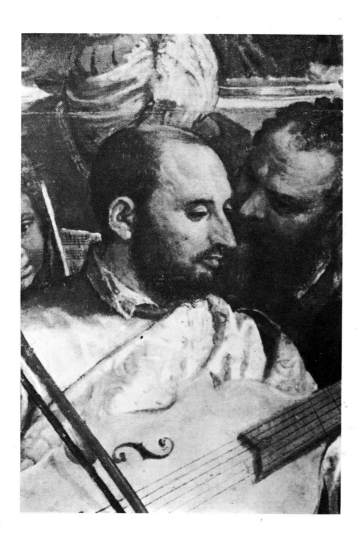

III   A Group of Musicians, Detail from the Feast

PARIS, Musée du Louvre.

Veronese plays a tenor viol in the left foreground (Plate IIIa) and Titian the double-bass on the right; the other instruments are (from the left) a trombone, another viol, a cornetto muto (it looks like a flute) and a violin. The music was suitable for a secular occasion and the hourglass poised in the centre of the table refers to Christ's response to his mother that: 'mine hour is not yet come'; that the musicians are Venetian painters underlines the analogy between the harmony of music and that of colour to which Vasari had alluded in the *Treatise on Painting* which preceded the 1550 edition of his *Lives*. That the heads included portraits was first noted by Boschini in 1674 and comparison with Agostino Carracci's, admittedly much later, engraving of Veronese (frontispiece) confirms that identification: Titian resembles his late self-portraits in Berlin and Madrid (Plate IIIb), but it is not possible to check that Jacopo Bassano plays the cornetto muto. Boschini is wrong in identifying the violinist as Tintoretto who is more likely to be shown playing the second viol next to Veronese; the bearded and foreshortened head fits with the self-portraits of Tintoretto in the Victoria and Albert Museum and the Louvre. The head of the man behind this group in a jester's hat with bells on looks like a slightly older version of the man on the right of the *Allegory of the Arts* now in the Capitoline Museum (Plate IIIc) whose plan identifies him as an architect. Since 1560 Palladio had been in charge of the rebuilding of the refectory at S. Giorgio Maggiore; if this figure is a portrait of Palladio it would express both Veronese's conviction about the relative merit of painting and architecture, and, no doubt, explain why Palladio should comment on many, to our eyes, dull decorative schemes in his villas but ignore those at Maser. No certain early portraits of Palladio survive, in spite of the identification proposed by C-A Isermeyer, *Festschrift Herbert Siebenhüner*, 1978, 137–142.

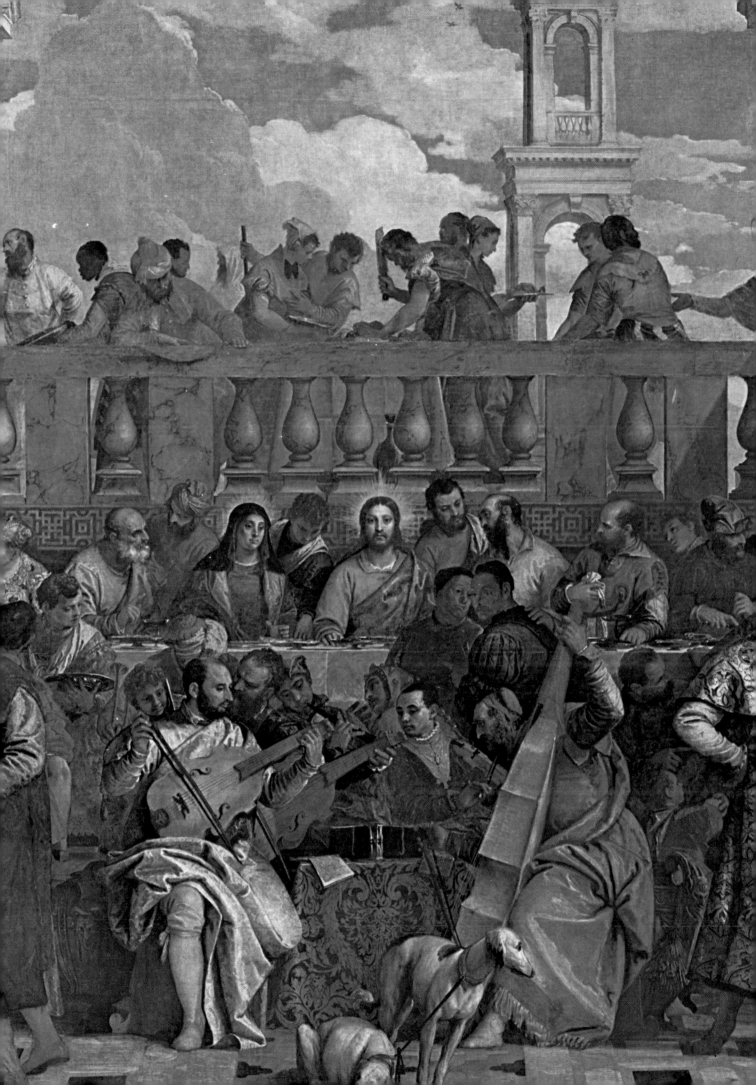

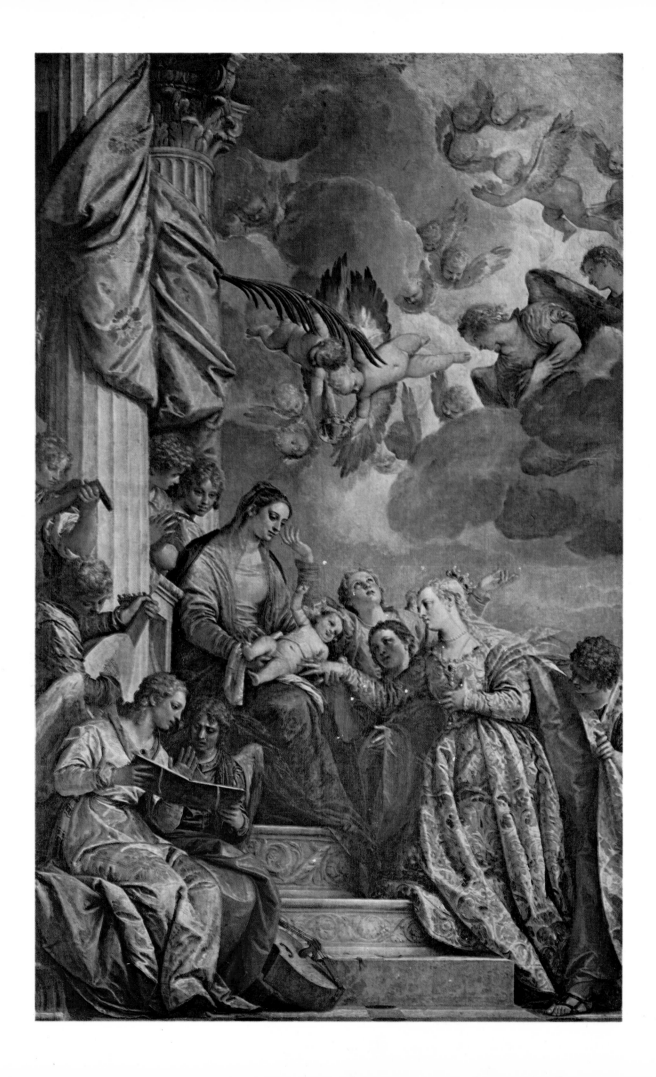

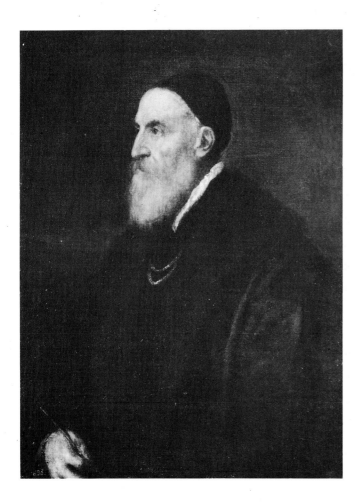

III b Titian
Self-Portrait
MADRID, Museo de Prado

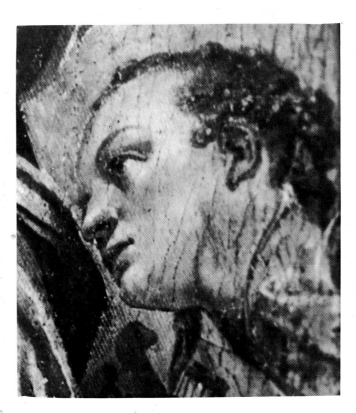

III c Alegory of the Arts, detail
ROME, Capitoline Muesuum

IV The Mystic Marriage of St. Catherine

VENICE, Gallerie dell'Accademia. 377 × 242 cm.

The picture, which was painted for the high altar of S. Caterina, passed to the Accademia in the Napoleonic period. The musical celebration of the saint's mystic marriage, which may have been suggested by the presence of a singing-gallery for the nuns in the church, develops from the altar in Detroit where an angel playing a cello on the left of the canvas balances the composition. The *Holy Family with SS. John the Baptist, Catherine and Theresa* in Brussels, which is difficult to judge for it is not properly displayed but which is probably autograph, may have served as the starting point for the development of the theme of the mystic marriage. This is echoed in the small picture formerly in the Hickox collection, now on loan to the Yale Art Gallery, where the heavens open behind the Virgin's head in celebration of the miracle; the Yale picture fits with a now lost *Virgin and Child with SS. John the Baptist, Catherine and Anne*, the best version of which appears to be that engraved by Barri, which must date from 1568 at the earliest, because that is the date on the letter from Castelfranco (now in Rotterdam, I. 40.) which Veronese turned over when he began the design.

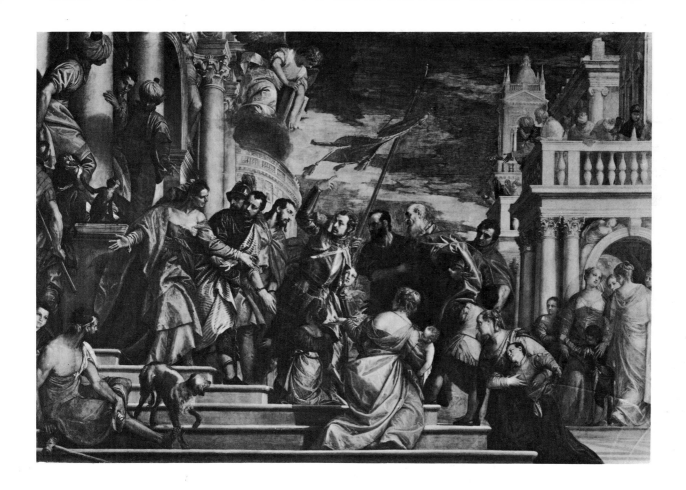

33 St. Sebastian exhorts SS. Mark and Marcellian to their Martyrdom

venice, S. Sebastiano. 355 × 450 cm.

This, the left hand of the two lateral altars in the main chapel, was probably part of the work for which Veronese received payment in 1565. The story is based on the *Golden Legend* like the *Martyrdom* opposite (Plate 34) which occurred after the efforts to shoot St. Sebastian to death with arrows had failed. The twins Mark and Marcellian were about to be martyred when they were begged not to, first by their mother, then by their father and finally by their wives with their children; St. Sebastian was present, still in the imperial army, and his eloquence, symbolized by his upraised arm and the bible carried by the angel, prevailed. The picture reworks the traditional formula employed by Carpaccio with a lower viewpoint and elegant architecture which is masked by the figures at the point where it would establish real depth; it may also be a critique in Venetian terms of Federico Zuccaro's *Raising of Lazarus* of about 1563 in the Grimani chapel in S. Francesco alla Vigna. The Zuccaro could have suggested both the composition and the gesture of the mother on the left who recalls the man with his arms spread wide in the *Lazarus* just as St. Sebastian's upraised arm may have been inspired by Christ's imperious gesture. The mother kneeling on the steps seen from the back and the careful alignment of the heads give Veronese's composition a fluency which contrasts with Zuccaro's comparatively isolated figures.

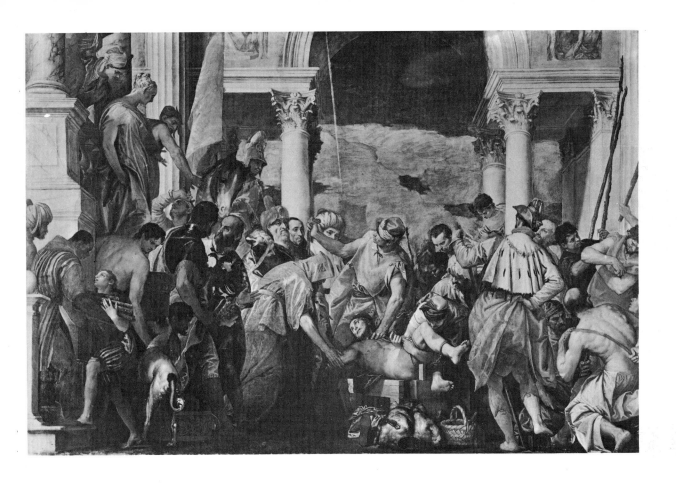

34 Martyrdom of St. Sebastian

VENICE, S. Sebastiano. 355 × 540 cm.

This, one of the two lateral canvases in the main chapel, was probably part of the work for which
Veronese received payment in 1565. The picture, which is on the right of the chapel, is lit from the
altar windows so that the group around the idol is in shadow, an extension of the formula first used
in Plate 12. The composition develops that of the *Martyrdom of SS. Primus and Felician* of 1562 now
in the Museo Civico, Padua; the extra attendants turn their backs on the spectator to concentrate
attention upon the saint whose twisting pose reflects that of the St. Lawrence in Titian's *Martyrdom
of St. Lawrence* in the Gesuiti (Plate 34a). The Serliana further emphasizes the saint by framing the.
main group, although the sky behind the figures has been radically altered by the oxidization
which has turned it brown.

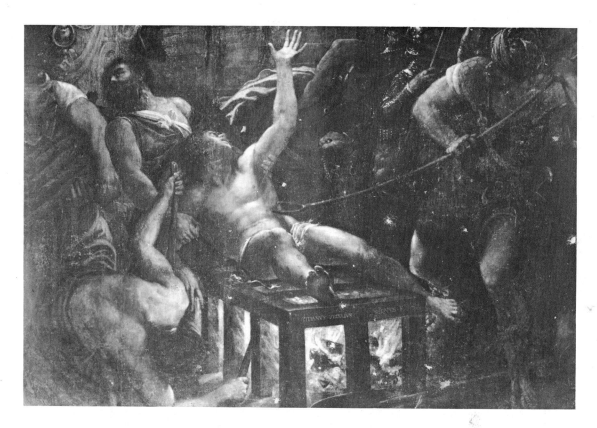

34a TITIAN
Martyrdom of St. Lawrence, detail
VENICE, Gesuiti.

35 Martyrdom of St. George

VERONA, S. Giorgio in Braida. 426 × 305 cm.

The vanishing point has been lowered to adjust to a spectator in the church but the canvas fits somewhat awkwardly into its frame. This, which may be a result of its removal at the orders of Napoleon in 1797 and subsequent return in 1815, suggests that the canvas was not painted in Verona, which Veronese visited in 1565 the year of his marriage to Badile's daughter, but in Venice. One of the drawings for the design (M.D. 1973, 138 ff.) bears the date 1565 on its verso which confirms the traditional dating of c. 1566. Veronese painted the *Miracle of St. Barnabas* now in Rouen for S. Giorgio at the same time; the moment chosen also shows his interest in the *Golden Legend* according to which St. Barnabas took the gospel of St. Matthew with him to Cyprus with which he cured the sick. The temple in the background of the Rouen canvas recalls Bramante's *Tempietto*, but the use of the Corinthian order suggests the example of the temple of Periptery that Palladio had designed for Book VI of Barbaro's edition of Vitruvius.

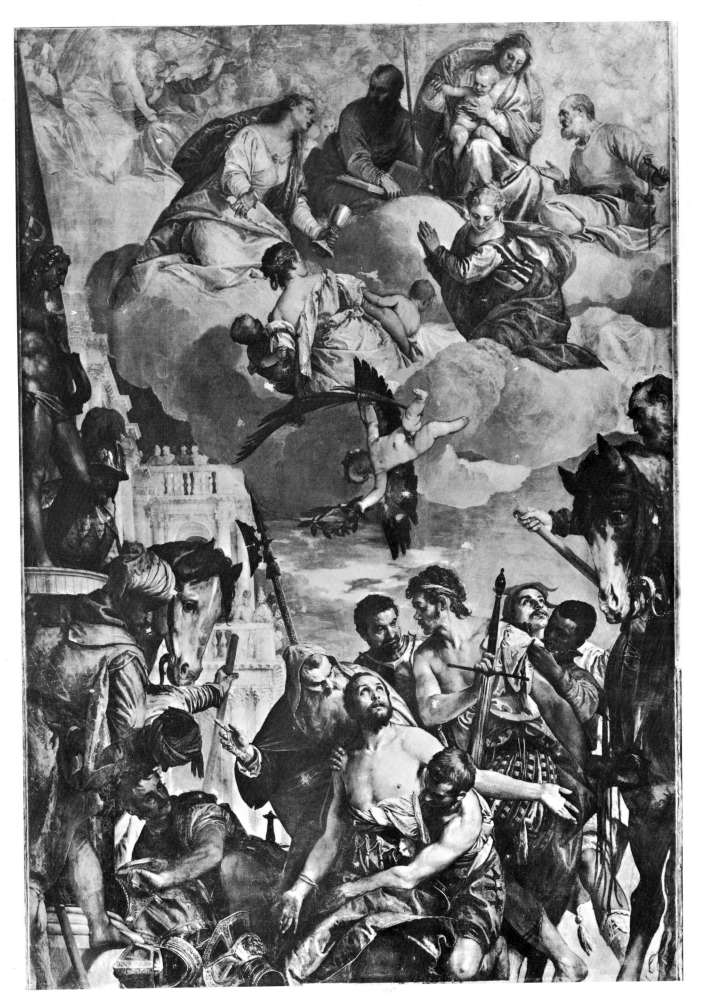

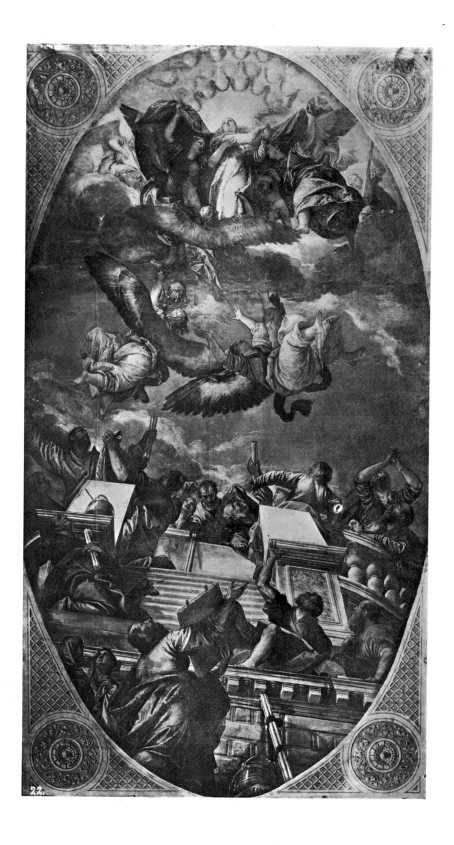

36 Assumption of the Virgin

VENICE, SS. Giovanni e Paolo, Cappella del Rosario. 762 × 432 cm.

This was the central oval of the ceiling of the Jesuit church of S. Maria dell'Umiltà which was completed by 1568, when Vasari referred to it. The ceiling included an *Annunciation* over the entrance and an *Adoration of the Shepherds* towards the altar. The three canvases were sent to Vienna in 1832 and returned in 1919; in 1926 they were placed in their present, anachronistic, frame which does not allow the spectator to stand back far enough to achieve the correct viewpoint. The *Assumption* was later reworked in the altar for Santa Maria Maggiore, now in the Accademia, which, in spite of the many doubts to the contrary, I believe to be basically autograph.

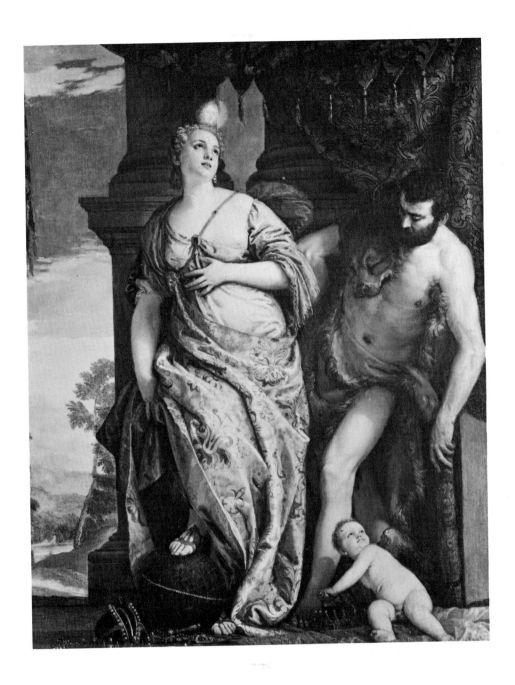

37 Omnia Vanitas

NEW YORK, Frick Collection. 214.6 × 167 cm.

This and the *Honor* were included in a list of paintings in Venice among the papers relating to Jacopo Strada in the Staatsarchiv, Munich. Strada was active on behalf of Albrecht V of Bavaria during 1567 when he made a number of purchases for the Bavarian Court. The picture's meaning, established by the biblical tag, refers to the vanity of love (Cupid), of the world, of jewels and of sceptres; the melancholic mood of Hercules as he looks at the globe associates him with these vanities and he probably represents a search for wisdom, a view which started with Mythographus III but with which Veronese may have been familiar through Bocchi's *Symbolicarum Quaestionum* (see P. 1977, 120 ff.). The woman appears to be excluded from the gloom and her attributes, the globe at her feet and the sun (the light of God) above her head identify her as Truth just as her upward glance and the gesture of her left arm underline her connection with Christian faith. The imagery fits with Albrecht's defence of the Catholic cause, and could be intended as a warning to his son and the young bride whom he married in 1568, not to value too highly the many costly jewels that they were given as wedding presents. It was subsequently no. 1212 in the 1621 Prague inventory of Rudolph II's collection; captured by the Swedes in 1648, it passed with Queen Christina to Rome; it was then in the Orléans collection in 1721 until sold in England to Thomas Hope in 1799. It was acquired by the present collection in 1912.

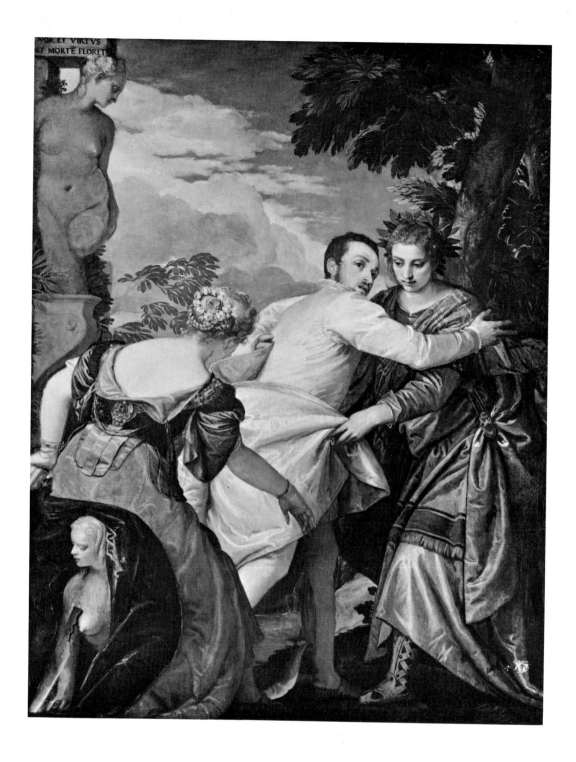

38 Honor Et Virtus Post Mortem Floret

NEW YORK, Frick Collection. 219 × 169.5 cm

This picture, like the *Omnia Vanitas*, was included in the list of paintings among Strada's papers and had the same subsequent history. The imagery is an adaptation of the Choice of Hercules, whose sense is given by the inscription; the lascivious lady on the left is death and the young man, presumably honour, escapes from her attentions into the arms of Virtue with nothing worse than a tear in his stockings. The picture may have been intended as a valedictory blessing on the young couple who were about to be married in 1568 by the forty-year old Elector, who intended their honour and virtue to flourish after his death. The laurel and the emphasis upon life and death in the two canvases echoes one of the *imprese* on the banners at the marriage; a lion seated under a laurel tree crowned himself with laurel decorated with diamonds and gold and the motto was 'IN VITA ET IN MORTE'.

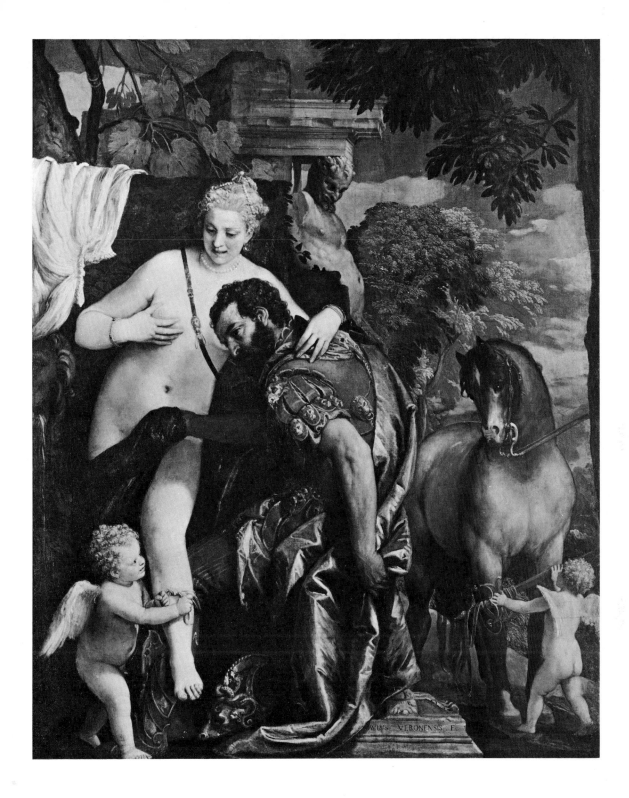

39 Mars and Venus Bound by Cupid

NEW YORK, Metropolitan Museum. 205.7 × 161 cm.

The picture is first certainly mentioned in the inventory of the Rudolph's collection in Prague drawn up by the Swedes in 1648, which also included another version of which only fragments survive. One of these pictures was no. 1151 in the 1621 inventory but it is impossible to decide which; its subsequent history was similar to that of Plate V except that it passed through a number of English private collections in the nineteenth century before being acquired by the museum in 1910. The contrast between the clothed Mars and the naked Venus goes back to a classical tradition which Mantegna had revived in the *Parnassus* now in the Louvre.

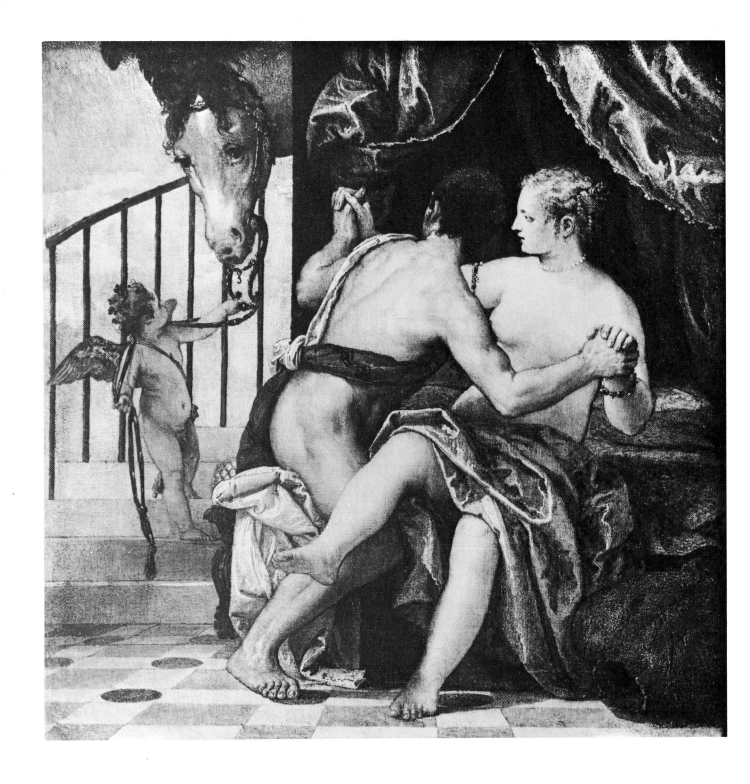

40   Mars and Venus

TURIN, Galleria Sabauda. 47 × 47 cm.

This is perhaps the wittiest of all Cinquecento paintings in its deflation of the suggestive mood of
the subject; the later version in Edinburgh shows Mars about the remove a shawl from Venus's
breasts but it too shares this defusion of the potential eroticism through Venus's smiling involvement
with Cupid at her feet. The picture which was first noted in the Orsetti collection was in that of
Faustino Lechi by 1768; it was bought by Richard Pryor in 1802 and subsequently appeared in the
sale of Sir Thomas Lawrence's collection. It was in an anonymous sale at Christies in 1907 and in
the Gualino collection, by whom it was presented to the Gallery, by 1924.

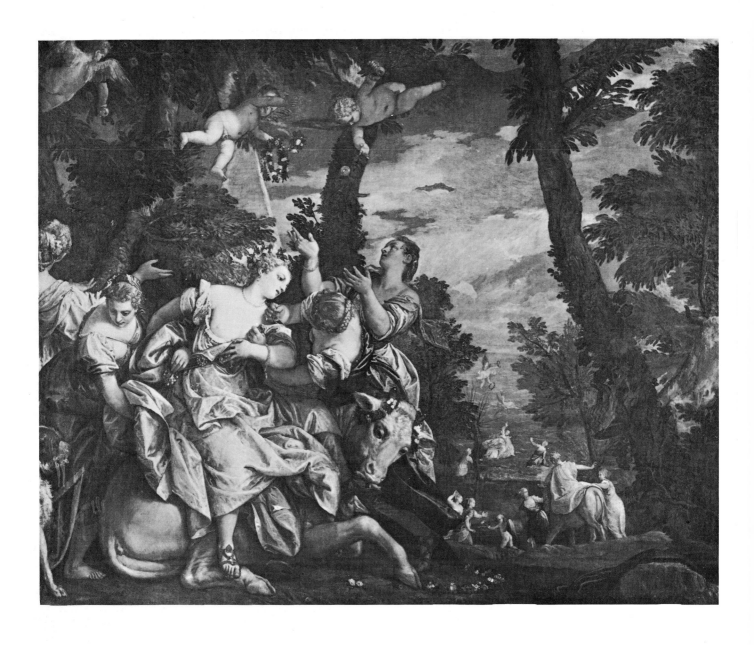

41 Rape of Europa

VENICE, Ducal Palace, Anticamera of the Sala del Collegio. 240 × 303 cm.

This, the prime version, was painted for Giacomo Contarini in 1573 (this is established by the drawing published by Deusch, P. 1968 295 ff.). It was presented to the Republic in 1713 and removed at the orders of Napoleon in 1797 to be returned in 1815. The picture is a reworking on a grander scale of the small canvas in the Rasini collection, Milan, which probably dates from the 1560s; it in turn inspired the version now in the Capitoline Galleries in which the studio seems to have played a larger part, although it needs to be cleaned. This must be the picture in the collection of Cardinal Carlo Pio to which del Sera referred in 1666 when he was trying to sell a variant to Cardinal Leopoldo de' Medici in Florence. Another large version was formerly in the Molino collection in Venice, where the Mantuan agents looked at it in 1662; Boschini tried to persuade Cardinal Leopoldo de' Medici to acquire it in 1665 but it was still in the collection in 1671.

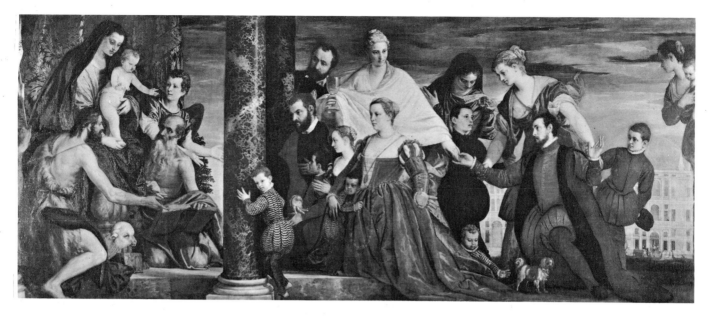

42 Virgin and Child with SS. John the Baptist, Jerome and the Coccina Family

DRESDEN, Gemäldegalerie. 167 × 416 cm.

The families of Alvise, Antonio and Zuanantonio Coccina are presented to the Holy Family by Faith, Hope and Charity while the saints and the angel in the background intercede on their behalf. The youngest child, Zuambattista, was born in c. 1570 while Antonio died in August 1572 which suggests that this, one of four paintings for the family, was painted in 1571. They were acquired for the ducal collection, Modena in 1645 and then by the Elector Frederick August III of Dresden in 1745. The family palace which had been built by Giacomo di Capponi by 1563 is shown in the background behind the families but the twin marble columns separate the Coccinas from the heavenly sphere, a sense of decorum that marks a development from the Louvre *Supper at Emmaus* (Plate 23). The immediate prototypes lie in the sixteenth century, Titian's lost *Votive Picture of Doge Andrea Gritti* and Tintoretto's *Virgin and Child with SS. Sebastian, Mark, Theodore and a Group of Treasurers* in the Accademia of 1567, but the clarity of the distinction between the earthly and heavenly zones may reflect Altichiero's *Members of the Cavalli Family Presented to the Virgin and Child* in S. Anastasia, Verona, although the architectural forms are very different.

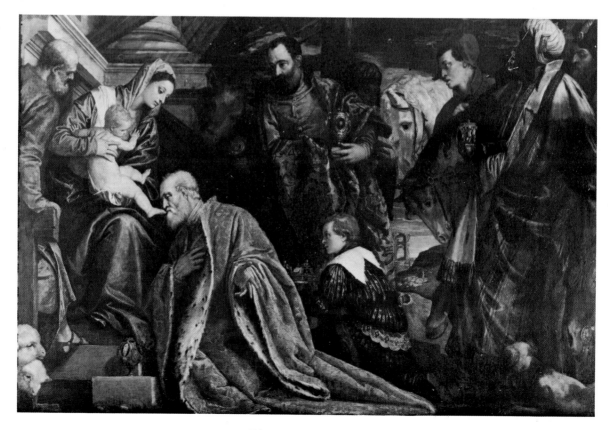

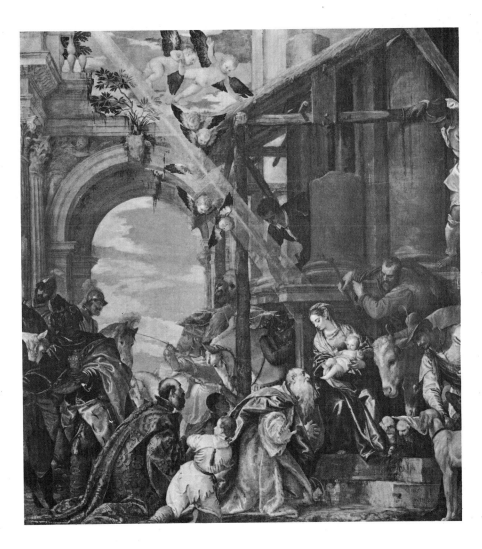

44 Adoration of the Magi

LONDON, National Gallery. 355 × 320 cm.

The picture, which is dated: 'M.D. LXXIII' was painted for S. Silvestro, Venice; it was taken
down when the church was remodelled in 1836–43, and was sold to Toffoli in 1855 from whom it
was purchased by the gallery in the same year. The picture extends and flattens the 'V' shape that
we noted on the left of the Chatsworth *Adoration* and concentrates attention upon the Virgin and
Child by making the magus to the left comparatively subdued, and by the burst of light.
Veronese's final variation on this theme is the great ceiling painting from S. Nicolò where the
design is reversed, the poses of the magi and their attendants are reworked as is the setting
and the viewpoint is foreshortened. There is a preparatory sketch for the S. Silvestro
painting in Haarlem, a chalk study for the second kneeling magus formerly in the Koenig collection
and a study for the negro servant in the Lehmann collection.

43 Adoration of the Magi

CHATSWORTH, Duke of Devonshire. 138.5 × 209 cm.

The picture is a reduced but probably autograph version of the canvas that Veronese painted for the
Coccina family in 1571 which the Duke of Devonshire acquired at the Duke of Portland's sale in
1725/26. The arms on the jug held by the central magus suggest that it might have been made for
the Donato family. The whole surface sparkles and the elegant shot silk of the magus to the right
and the pale pink brocade of the one who kneels and kisses Christ's feet are set off against the rich
red of the central magus. The composition, like that of the *Rape of Europa* (Plate 41) combines a
frieze-like grouping, which is broken by the view of the ruins in the distance, with the 'V' of the
Holy Family and leading two magi. The earliest version in this series is probably the small canvas
now in the Hermitage, which was in the collection of Pierre Crozat by 1740, whose brilliant
colours fit with those of the paintings of the 1560s.

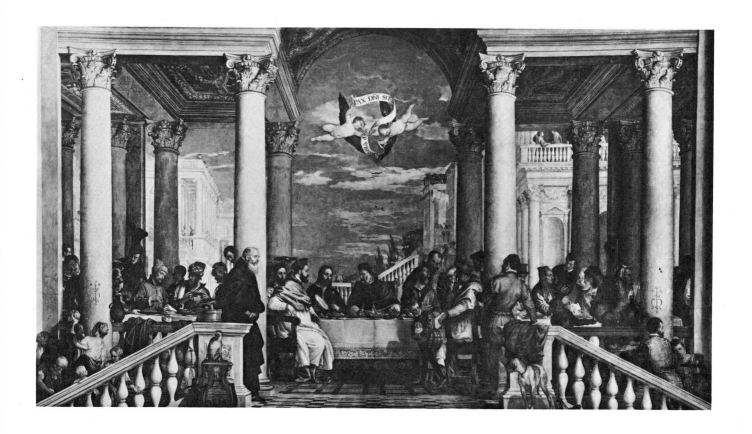

45   Feast of St. Gregory the Great

VICENZA, Monte Berico. 477 × 862 cm.

According to the *Golden Legend* St. Gregory, when Pope, invited pilgrims to dine with him; when he turned to one whose hands he wanted to wash he disappeared. That night Christ appeared in vision to tell him that he had been the guest. The action is concentrated at the moment of the feast and Christ's simple gesture of raising the dish reveals the miracle to the saint. The recent cleaning, which reveals the terrible damage caused by the Austrians in 1848 who cut the picture first into 5 or 6 large pieces and then into 32 smaller ones, shows that the emphasis of the colour is upon the dark red of St. Gregory's robe which is set off by the green of Christ's mantel and framed by the pale pink costumes of the two flanking cardinals. The miracle is further emphasized by the inscription borne by the angels: 'PAX DNI SIT SEP BISCU', which alludes to the mass that St. Gregory celebrated in S. Maria Maggiore when an angel gave the response: 'Et cum spiritu tuo' to the Pope's 'Pax Domini'. The picture, which was painted in Venice in 1572, was removed to the Brera in 1798, but never got to Paris being returned to Vicenza in 1817. After the Austrian damage it was reassembled and cleaned in the 1850s and again at the time of the Palladio exhibition in Vicenza in 1973.

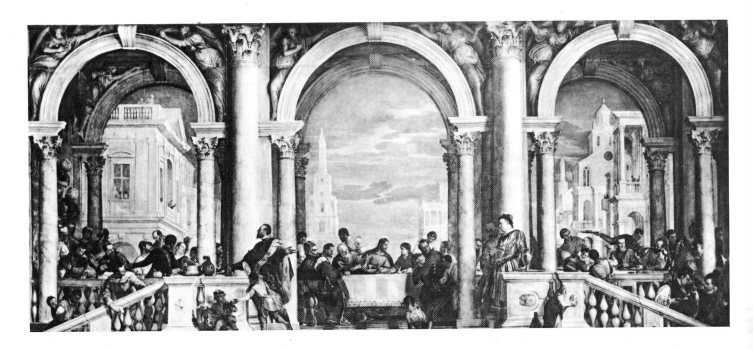

46 Feast in the House of Levi

VENICE, Gallerie dell'Accademia. 555 × 1280 cm.

The picture which is inscribed: 'A.D. MDLXXIII DIE XX APR' and 'FECIT. D. COVI MAGNU LEVI LUCAE CAP V' was painted for the refectory of SS. Giovanni e Paolo to replace a *Last Supper* by Titian which had been destroyed by fire in 1571. Veronese appeared before the inquisition to answer questions about the picture on the 18th July 1573 (the text is transcribed by Fehl, *Gazette des Beaux Arts*, 1961, 325 ff.); the outcome was a compromise for the picture does not fit with the passage in Luke, which was later the subject of a dull picture by his heirs from the refectory of S. Jacopo on the Giudecca, now in the Palazzo del Gran Guardia, Verona. The inscription takes care to back-date the new title to April, when the picture must first have been unveiled. The earlier versions of the *Feast in the House of Simon*, which I believe to have been the original choice of scene, are Plate 27, the painting in the Brera, from the refectory of S. Sebastiano and the picture at Versailles from the Servite church. The action fuses the accounts of Matthew 26, who describes all the apostles as discussing the Magdalen's action and of John 12 where Martha is referred to and the Magdalen anoints Christ's feet rather than his head. For the two later versions Veronese returned to John according to whose gospel only Judas protested and the scene was set in the house of Martha and Mary (making no mention of Simon, who is retained in both versions); Judas is shown isolated from the other apostles in the position usually reserved for him in Last Suppers and Martha is brought into greater prominence.

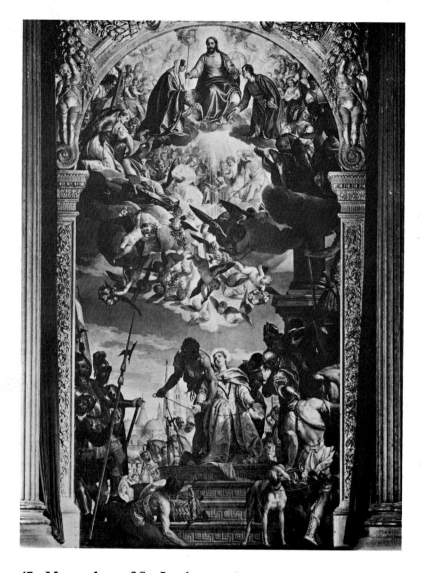

47 Martyrdom of St. Justina

PADUA, S. Giustina. 525 × 240 cm.

The picture, as Ridolfi noted, is almost invisible because of the poor lighting on the main altar of the church of S. Giustina, which had been commenced in 1509, and was finished in c. 1580. The altar was built in 1560 and Veronese together with his brother Benedetto (who in spite of the popular view to the contrary can have had little to do with the present canvas) is documented as present in Padua in 30 March 1575; by the 27 October of that year he had entered into an agreement with the monks of S. Giustina to provide them with an altar for the Church of Conca, by which date he had, presumably, completed the present altar. The choice of moment with the saint kneeling in intercession to the Deësis does not follow the legend of her martyrdom, which is celebrated on October 7th, but appears to be inspired by the *Martyrdom of St. George* (Plate 35). Veronese's awareness of the legend is shown by the canvas in the Uffizi which follows the narrative closely and which inspired the school painting now in the Museo Civico, Padua. Both the Uffizi painting and the Vatican *St. Helen* appear to be close in date to the *Martyrdom of St. Justina*.

V Mercury, Herse and Aglauros

CAMBRIDGE, Fitzwilliam Museum. 232 × 173 cm.

The early history of this canvas is unknown; it was no. 1193 in the 1621 Prague inventory of Rudolph II's collection; its subsequent history was similar to that of Plate 37 except that it was bought by Lord Fitzwilliam who bequeathed it to the museum in 1816. The choice of the climactic moment in Ovid's account in Book II of the *Metamorphoses* is unusual; Pordenone had shown the earlier moment when the flying Mercury first sees Herse on the facade of Palazzo d'Ana that is recorded in a drawing in the Victoria and Albert Museum and the illustrated editions of Ovid, exemplified by the woodcut that accompanied Dolce's 1553 translation, showed the first encounter between Aglauros and Mercury outside the palace.

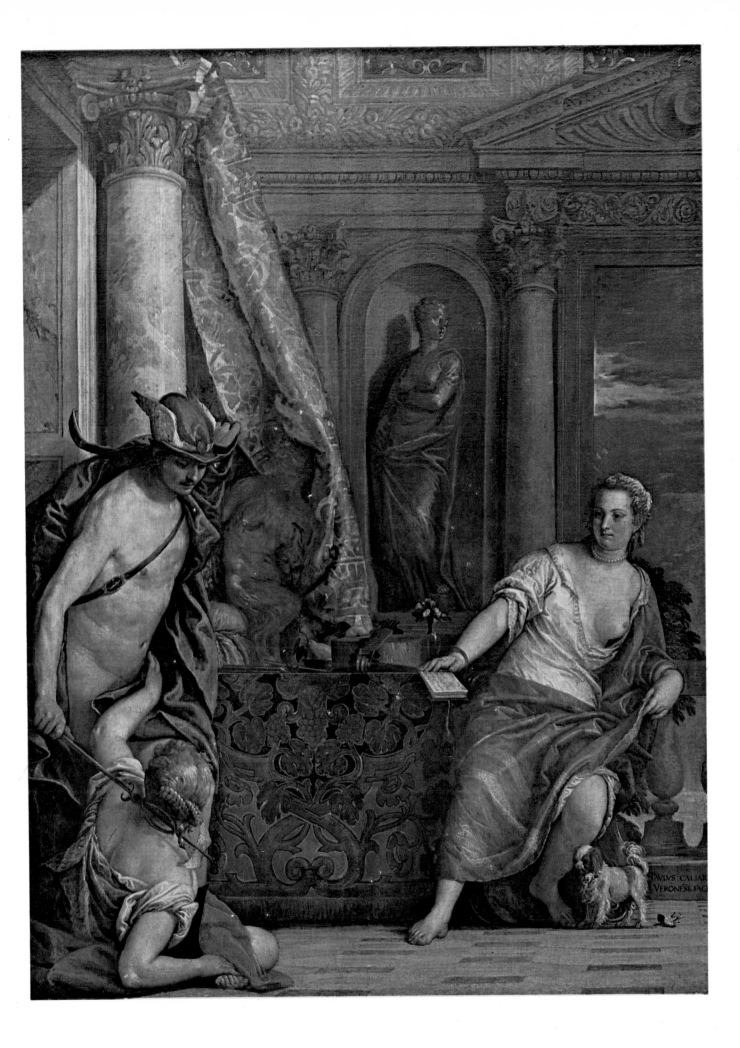

PAVLVS CALIARI
VERONESI FAC

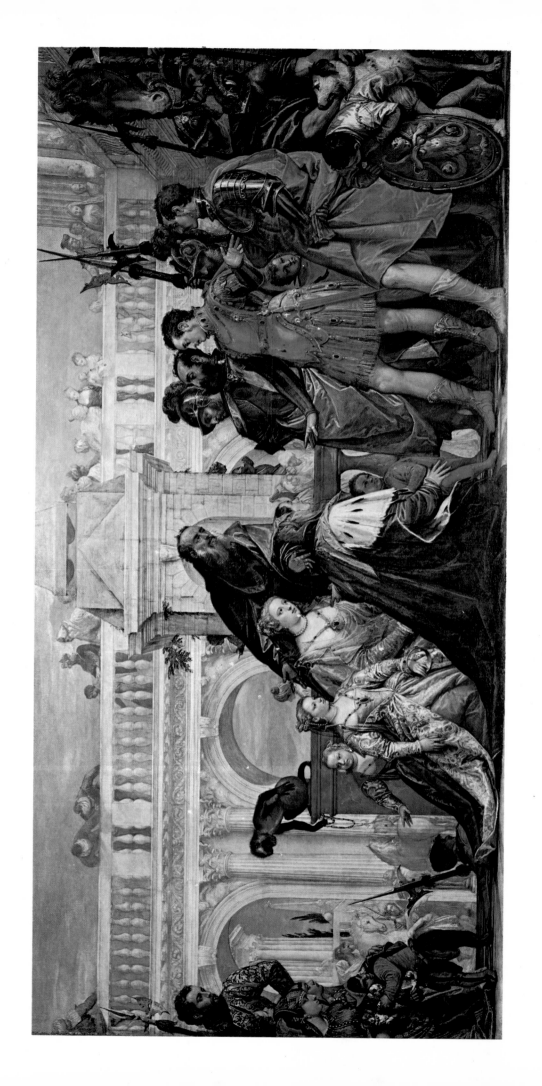

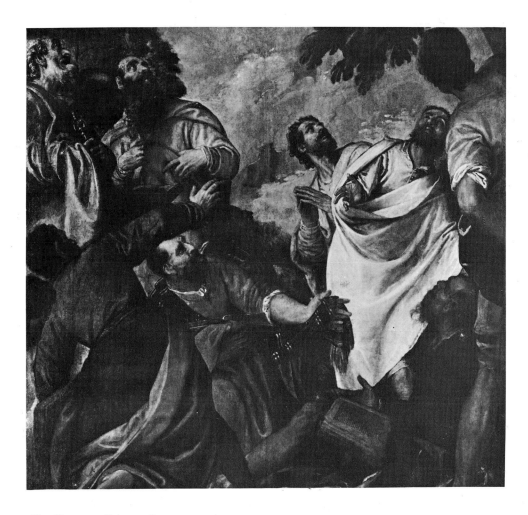

48 Group of Apostles

PRAGUE, Narodni Gallery. 243 × 192 cm.

This is the bottom section of the *Ascension of Christ* which Laura Cumana commissioned for S. Francesco, Padua in 1575, and which was replaced by a copy by Pietro Damino in 1625. The photomontage (Plate 48a) replaces the apostles under the Christ, of the *Ascension* which is difficult to see in the church now that it has been removed from the fifth chapel on the left to the entrance wall. The *Apostles* were in the Arundel collection by 1655; Thomas Howard, Earl of Arundel had been active purchasing in Italy in c. 1615–17. They were owned by Franz von Imstanraed in 1667 and by the Bishop of Liechtenstein at Oloumec in 1680; they were part of the collection of Castle Kromeriz which the state acquired in 1930. The small canvas of the *Ascension* in the Capitoline Galleries, which is difficult to judge because of damage, is probably an autograph variant whose function is uncertain. The early history of the *Apostles* was established by Safarik, *Saggi e Memorie di Storia dell'Arte*, 1968, 79 ff.

VI The Family of Darius before Alexander

LONDON, National Gallery, 236 × 474 cm.

The picture was first recorded in the collection of Francesco Pisani in 1648; it remained in the family collection as one of the most famous pictures in Venice until its sale to the gallery in 1857. It has been suggested that the improprieties in the setting and the costumes reflect the influence of Renaissance theatre (Rosand, A.B. 1973, 217 ff.). In the text we argue that it is intended to celebrate a second Alexander and suggest the possibility that this might be Francesco's great-uncle, Pietro, who died without having married and whose property could have reverted to his brother's family, although we do not unfortunately know for whom the picture was commissioned and there is no guarantee that it was a member of the Pisani family. Such a comparison with Alexander would have seemed in place after the Battle of Lepanto since contemporaries compared the dead Venetians with the greatest of the ancients. See also Cecil Gould, *The Family of Darius before Alexander* by Paolo Veronese, 1978, who argues that it was painted for the Pisani palace at Este, a view that is open to objection, see B.M. 1978 325 ff.

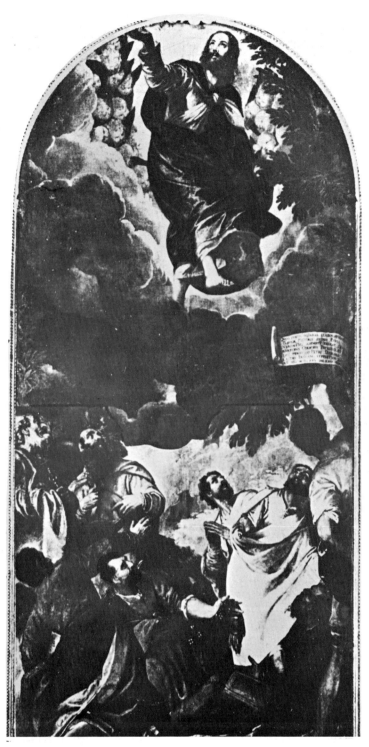

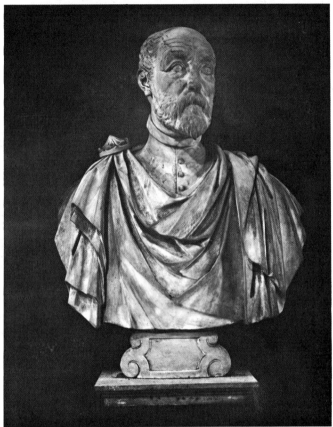

49a Bust of Alessandro Vittoria

VENICE, S. Zaccaria.

49 Portrait of Allessandro Vittoria

NEW YORK, Metropolitan Museum. 110 × 77 cm.

The picture, which was sold from the Brownlow collection at Christies in 1923 was bought by the museum from an Italian collector in 1946. The identification, first proposed by A. M. Frankfurter, is supported by a comparison with the bust on Vittoria's tomb in S. Zaccaria (Plate 49a) and by the fact that the *modello* of St. Sebastian that he holds relates to Vittoria's bronze in the Metropolitan Museum. Vittoria cast bronze St. Sebastians in 1566 and 1575; comparison with his portrait by Morone, now in Vienna, which has convincingly been dated to 1552–53, shows him as much older and the New York portrait is therefore likely to date from 1575. Veronese had worked with Vittoria in the 1550s both at Maser and at Palazzo Trevisan and the expressive possibilities of the St. Sebastian influenced his own version of this figure on the right of Plate 51.

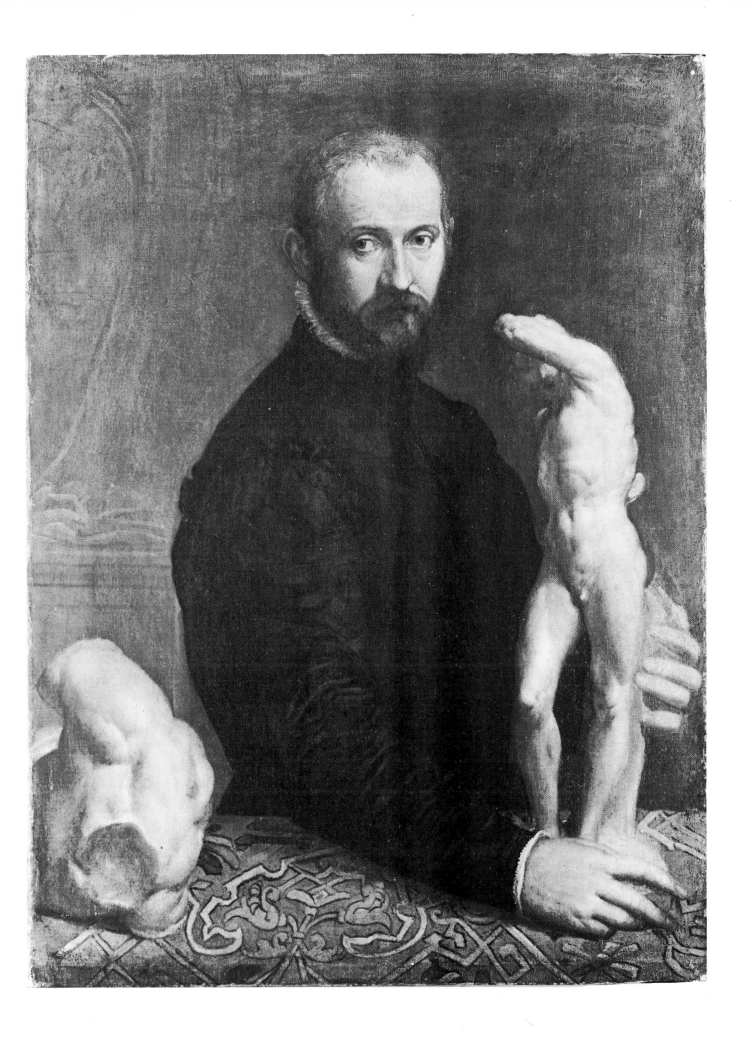

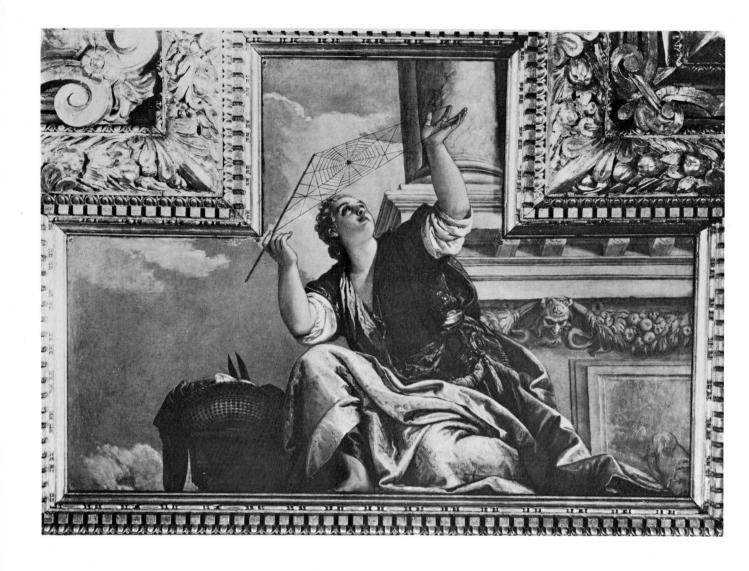

50 Justice and Peace before Venice: Industry

VENICE, Palazzo Ducale, Sala del Collegio. 250 × 180 cm., and 150 × 220 cm. respectively.

The decoration of the Sala del Collegio was destroyed by fire in 1574 and the redecoration began at once. Veronese received his first payment in December 1575, although the account book breaks off in 1577, before the final payment. *Justice and Peace* was over the Tribunal with *Faith* in the centre and *Mars and Neptune* towards the doors. These allegories have both a general and a specific application to the Collegio which was responsible for the business of the Senate (the supreme legislative body); *Justice and Peace* alludes to this function, *Mars and Neptune* refers to its role as the Ministry of War and *Faith* to its responsibility for religion. These canvases were accompanied by pairs of allegorical ladies; reading from the entrance they are: *Liberality* (the eagle giving up a feather) and *Fortune* (holding out the dice); *Industry* (Plate 50) (the spiders' reputation for never ceasing to work goes back to Isidore of Seville) and *Moderation* (this identification of the character of the ermine, that of the *Fior di Virtù*, seems more relevant in the context of the scheme than the alternative association with chastity); *Vigilance* (the crane) and *Mildness* (the lamb, equated with the lamb of god); *Felicitas Publica* (the Caduceus and cornucopia derived from classical coinage) and *Faith* (the dog, most faithful of animals). The need for the members of the Collegio to cultivate these virtuous ends is obvious and the message of the central canvases was reinforced by a series of grisaille classical histories.

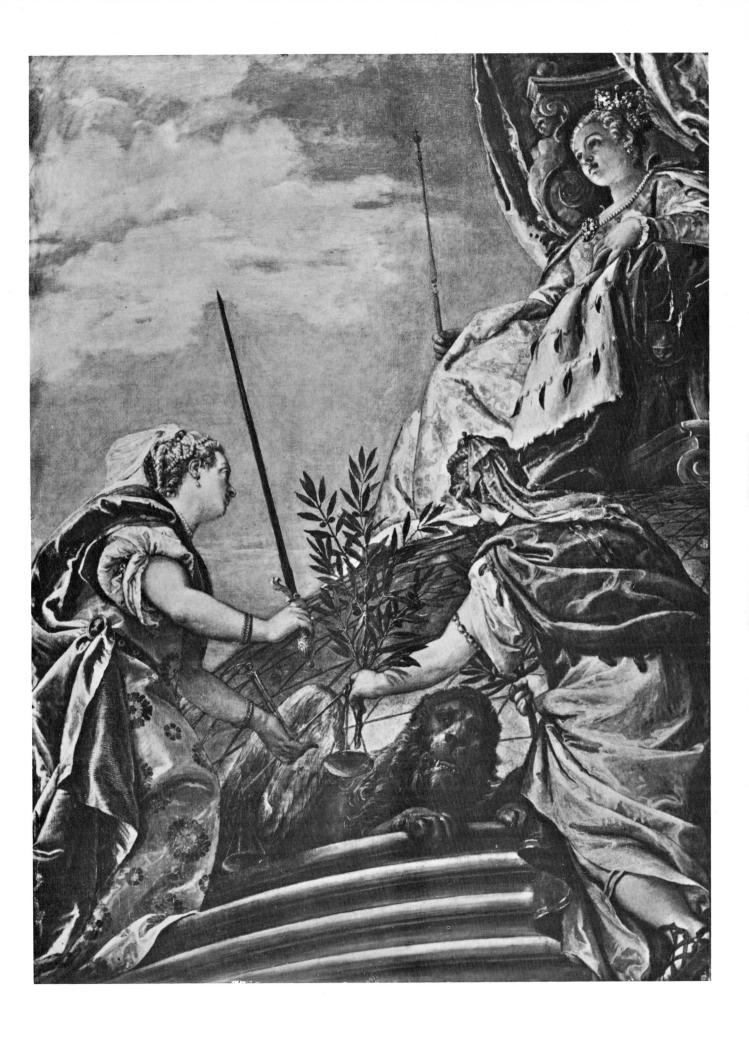

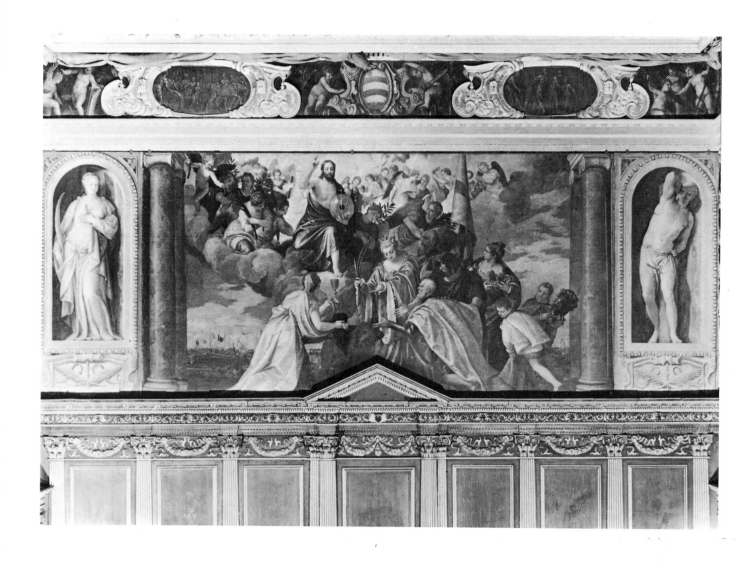

51 Doge Sebastiano Venier's Thanksgiving for the Battle of Lepanto

VENICE, Palazzo Ducale, Sala del Collegio. 285 × 565 cm.

Sebastiano Venier had been elected Doge in 1577 but died in March 1578, which must be the dates for
the commission of this painting; he had been one of the commanders at the Battle of Lepanto
on 7 October 1571 and his votive painting recalls that great victory over the Turks. He kneels
before S. Justina (on whose saint's day the battle occurred and who is also one of the flanking
saints—the other St. Sebastian is Venier's namesake) and the lion of Venice in worship of Christ
who is accompanied by angels while in the background we see the naval battle. To the left Faith
kneels with her back to us holding the chalice while St. Mark introduces the Doge; between them
can be seen Agostino Barbarigo, the Venetian Proveditor Generale at the battle, while Venice is
behind them on the right with two attendants. Sinding-Larsen, J.W.C.I. 1956, 298 ff., noted that
the early description of the painting by Sansovino fitted the *modello* in the British Museum, not the
composition as executed and argued that the changes in the present canvas were the work of a later
artist. Veronese, however worked with considerable freedom in the *Venice Triumphant* (Plate 50) and
the plan described by Sansovino must have been felt to be inadequate because the victory was one
for the whole of Christendom, not just Venice, and so Christ was a more suitable figure to receive
the Doge's thanksgiving than St. Mark. This change further emphasizes the sacramental nature of
the chalice, a theme of other late Veronese's, notably Plate 54. The *modello* reveals Veronese's share
in the changes for in it Agostino Barbarigo is added as an afterthought over the flag between
St. Mark and Venice, and St. Justina also appears to have been added later.

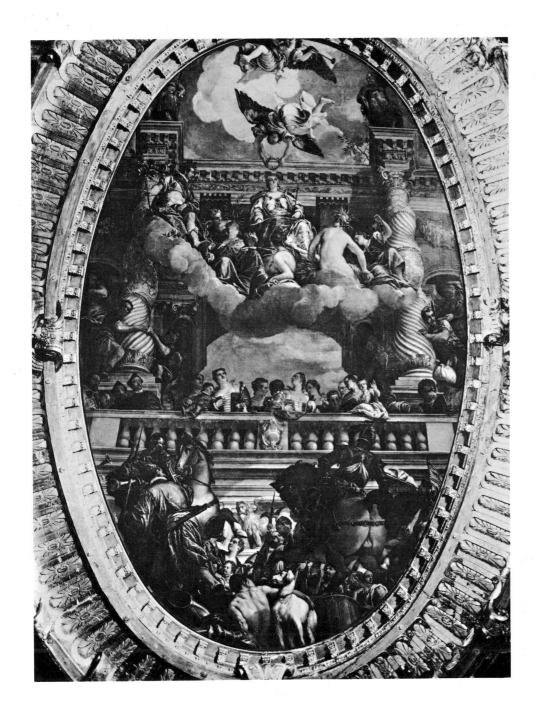

52   Venice Triumphant

VENICE, Palazzo Ducale, Sala del Gran Consiglio. 904 × 580 cm.

The original decoration of the ceiling, which was destroyed by fire in December 1577, was replaced by a framework designed by Cristoforo Sorte which was under way by August 1579, and the scheme of the decoration was drawn up in the same month (see Wolters, M.K.I.F., 1965/66, 271 ff.): Veronese's ceiling paintings which were under way by 1582 were completed by 1584. *Venice Triumphant* is flanked by two further canvases the *Conquest of Smyrna by Paolo Mocenigo* and the *Defence of Scutari by Antonio Loredano*, which are darker and more sombre in their handling, much of which can be attributed to the workshop, a development that echoes the way in which the darker flanking canvases in the ceiling from S. Nicolò contrast with the rich *Adoration* in the centre. This was intentional for on the verso of the Oxford drawing for the *Conquest* is a badly drawn oval, which reflects the frame of the *Venice Triumphant*. In the *modello* for the ceiling, which is now in the collection of Lord Harewood, guide lines were ruled on the sheet, the architecture was drawn next and the figures added at the last stage; there are many minor changes between the *modello* and the final canvas, one of which, the lower curve of the main arch, is indicated in the drawing.

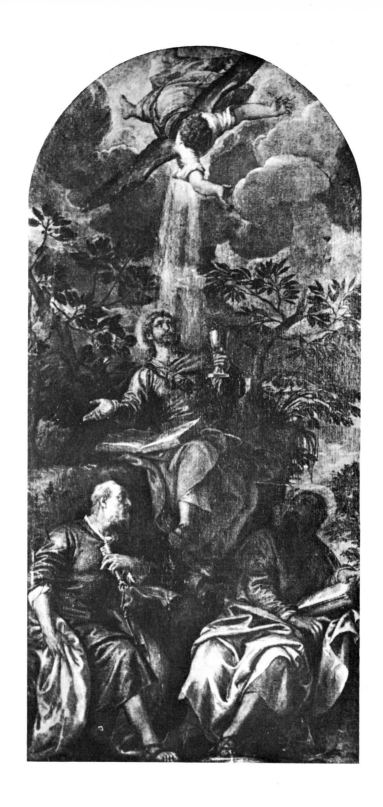

53 SS. Peter, Paul and John the Evangelist

VENICE, S. Pietro. 320 × 155 cm.

This, the most romantic of all Veronese's altars was painted at the commission of Giovanni Trevisan, the 13th Patriarch of Venice, for the altar which he dedicated to St. John the Evangelist in his church of S. Pietro, Castello; both altar and altarpiece were completed by 1581. The landscape setting, the sombre colour, expressive figures and visionary quality of the angel's response to the upheld chalice make this very different from the earlier versions of enthroned saints: the *St. Anthony Abbot Enthroned* in the Brera from S. Antonio Torcello of c. 1570 (the year that the decision was taken to gild the altars), the *SS. Lawrence, Jerome and Prospero* painted for the Malipiero family chapel in S. Giacomo dell'Orio in 1573, and the Verbosca polyptich of the mid-1570s.

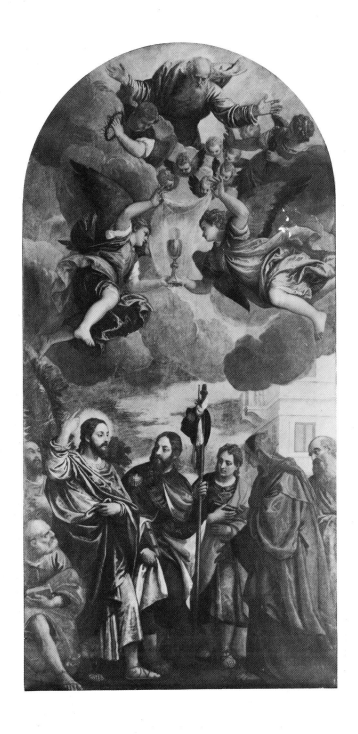

54 Christ with Zebedee's Wife and Sons

STAMFORD, Burghley House, 270 × 150 cm.

The picture, which was painted as the main altar of S. Giacomo, Murano probably in the late 1570s was acquired by the 9th Earl of Exeter in 1769, together with the *SS. James and Augustine* from the organ shutters. Both the altar and the organ shutters, which were completed by a now lost *Mystic Marriage of St. Catherine*, are, in spite of the doubts to the contrary expressed by Italian critics, autograph. The choice of subject is unprecedented in Venetian painting and connects both with the picture's function as the main altar in a church dedicated to St. James and with the Catholic devotion to the host. The S. Giacomo altar inspired the full-length version in Grenoble, one of the pictures that Bernini disliked on his visit to Paris in 1665, where the weight and complexity of Christ's robe fits with that of the paintings in the 1570s and the stance and gesture of Zebedee's wife are adapted from that of the Stamford painting. The Grenoble painting in its turn appears to have been the starting-point for the apostle with one arm behind his back, the gesture of Zebedee's wife and the Christ in the half-length version now in the Chrysler collection. The Chrysler painting was probably in the collection of Sir Gregory Page, London in 1761 (as *Christ with a Woman Taken in Adultery*, the title under which it was sold at Sotheby in 1957, and dimensions of 112 × 158 cm.).

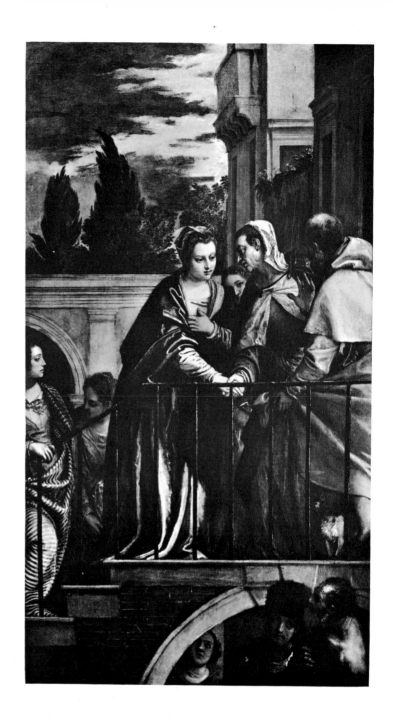

55　The Visitation

BIRMINGHAM, Barber Institute. 272 × 152·5 cm.

The picture, one of those painted for S. Giacomo, Murano, was prepared in a drawing formerly in
the Koenig collection, Haarlem which included sketches for the Charity that flanked the
Annunciation in the Confraternity of the Mercanzia. Charity is further elaborated on another sheet
(see B.M., 1971 p. 733) with drawings for the SS. Justina and Sebastian of Plate 51 of 1577 and
1578; this must be the date of the present painting and of the other canvases from S. Giacomo
which include Plate 54 and the *Resurrection* in Westminster Hospital, London. The present canvas
was acquired by Lord Clive from Sir James Wright in 1771 and was bought by the gallery in 1953.
The action is set on one of the small stone bridges that are a feature of Venice which may have
been inspired by that in the background of Palma Vecchio's version in Vienna; it creates space in
the foreground for the spectators who witness a *Visitation* carried through with expressive gestures
that are matched by the sombre tonality. Both these features recur in the *Thanksgiving of St. Ann
and Joachim* in S. Polo where Joachim and Ann kneel in adoration of the image of the Virgin
which is borne by the angels. The picture, completed by 1581 has suffered but, like the *Visitation*,
is most probably autograph.

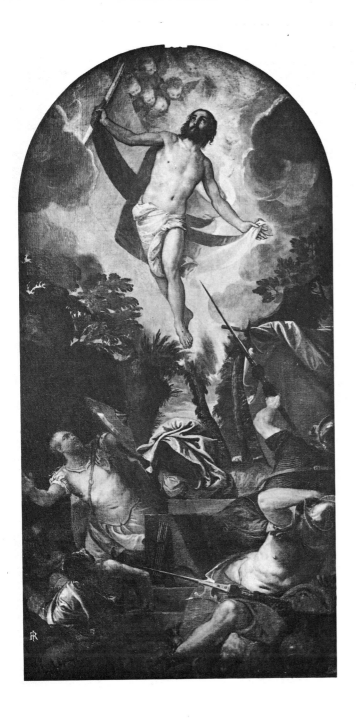

56　Resurrection

VENICE, S. Francesco alla Vigna. 325 × 160 cm.

The picture, which has remained *in situ* in the Badoer chapel in S. Francesco alla Vigna, cannot be dated precisely but it was certainly finished by 1584 and is probably close in date to the version from S. Giacomo, now in the Westminster Hospital, which probably shares the date of 1577 to 1578 of Plate 55. The drama is conveyed by the contrapposto of the soldier in the foreground and by the expressive figure of Christ on whom attention is focussed by the burst of light over the screen of trees. The earliest *Resurrection* by Veronese is the small canvas in Dresden which fuses motifs from Titian's Brescia and Urbino versions of this subject, and uses colour typical of the 1560s in the contrast of the red of Christ's robe with the green sky. In its background the three Maries approach the empty sepulchre guarded by two angels, and this may well have suggested the otherwise unprecedented appearance of the two angels holding the top of the tomb in the Westminster Hospital version, a motif which at the same date, 1577 to 1581, Tintoretto used in his canvas in the Scuola Grande of S. Rocco. The S. Francesco altar, whose execution has been wrongly doubted, was later to inspire Annibale Carracci's version of this subject, now in the Louvre.

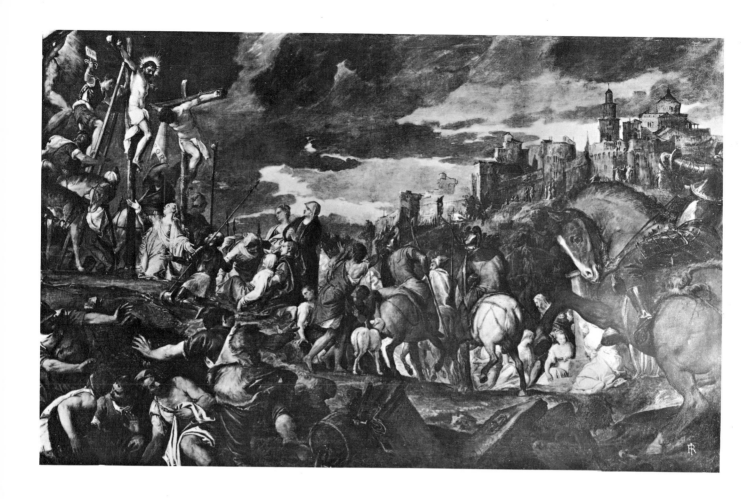

57 Crucifixion

VENICE, Accademia. 287 × 447 cm.

This great, and slightly abraded canvas, is one of the series of paintings by Veronese and his workshop from S. Nicolò ai Frari, which were most probably painted in c. 1582, the date of the consecration of the church. It passed to the Accademia in 1834. The composition with the view of Jerusalem in the distance recalls that of his *Defence of Scutari* on the ceiling of the Sala del Gran Consiglio in the Palazzo Ducale on which he was working in 1582 and derives from Titian's *Battle of Cadore* that was destroyed by the fire in the Palace in 1577. Veronese transformed the design in two smaller canvases, one formerly in Dresden and another in the Louvre. The Dresden canvas, one of those destroyed in the last war, is as dramatic as the S. Nicolò altar with the burst of light on Christ, the Magdalen hanging onto the bottom of the cross and the centurion kneeling in recognition of Christ. The Louvre version substitutes a mood of poignance for the drama of the other two canvases, with a richer display of colour, notably in the Magdalen's yellow cloak as she hides her head in grief. Another large scale version, about whose provenance little is known, is in store at the Pitti; the composition with Christ isolated in the centre by the ladders recalls Tintoretto's *Crucifixion* in the Albergo of the Scuola of S. Rocco; it needs cleaning but it may be, at worst, an outstanding workshop product.

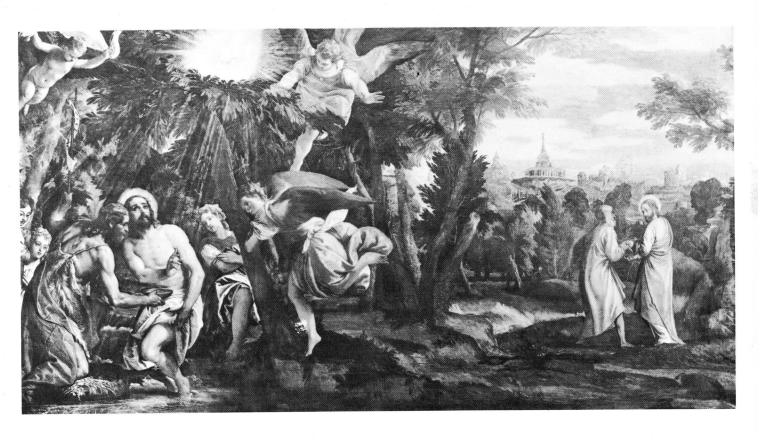

58 Baptism of Christ

MILAN, Brera. 248 × 450 cm.

This is another of the canvases from S. Nicolò ai Frari, which like Plate 57, was probably painted
in 1582 and passed to the museum in 1809. The 1561 *Baptism* in the Sacristy of the Redentore
concentrates upon the drama of the figures with the heavens opening behind Christ in a way
which is similar to the paintings from S. Benedetto Po (Plates 28 and 28a). The next version, that in
Latisana, of 1567 was nearly twice as large as the Redentores canvas but this alone does not explain
the new importance given to the trees which fill over half the canvas and open in the centre to a
vista of mountains; they derive from the landscape in Titian's *Death of St. Peter Martyr* and this new
feeling for figures set against a screen of trees recurs in the Sarasota *Rest on the Flight* of 1572, and
the *Rape* (Plate 41) of 1573. The other versions of the *Baptism* were upright canvases, that from S.
Nicolò was rectangular which must explain the inclusion of the next episode, the temptation. The
final painting in the series is the *Baptism* in the Uffizi which was painted for S. Giovanni in Malta
(the provenance, which is often questioned, was established by Ludwig, *Jahrbuch der Kunsthistorischen
Sammlungen des allerhöchsten Kaiserhauses*, 1901, second part p. 11 and XX) in 1587, the date on the
verso of a drawing at Harvard which, together with another at Edinburgh, relate to this canvas.
None of the other versions of the subject are, in my view, autograph.

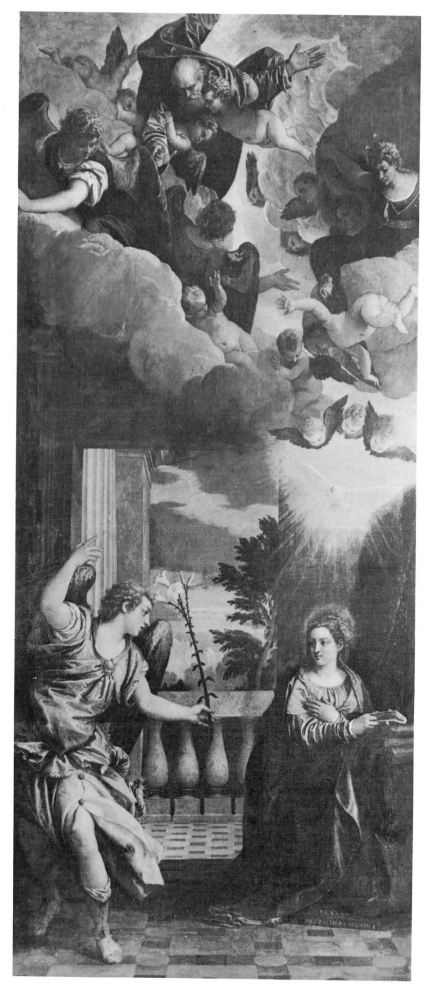

94

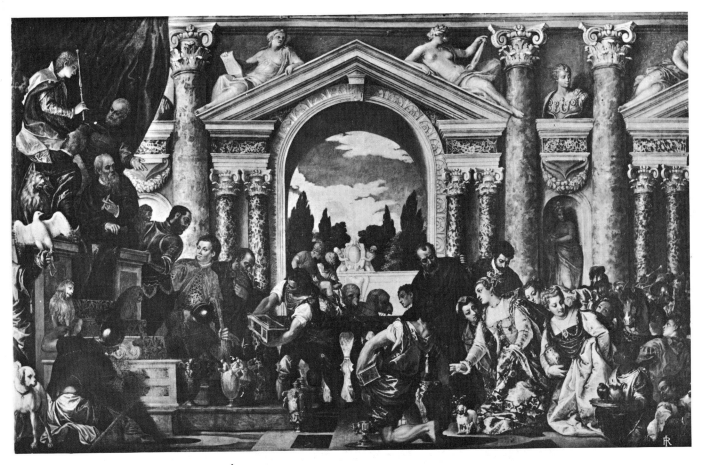

60   The Queen of Sheba before Solomon

TURIN, Galleria Sabauda. 344 × 545 cm.

This great painting must have been painted for the youthful Charles Emanuel I between his accession to the Dukedom of Savoy in 1580 and 1584. The type of flattery used in the picture is not new, in 1559 the Flemish artist Lucas de Heere produced a version of the subject in which the Solomon is a portrait of Philip II of Spain; Veronese's approach is subtler for the youthful Solomon alludes to Emanuel without (to judge from his coins) being a portrait. The flattery was continued in the now lost *Adoration of the Magi*, a picture traditionally coupled with the *Queen of Sheba* just as Charles Emanuel must have appeared as the paragon of the youthful warrior-hero in the *David with the Head of Goliath* commissioned at the same time together with a *Judith*. Ruskin's enthusiasm for the canvas, which needs cleaning, is preferable to the modern view which sees here the hand of Benedetto.

59   The Annunciation

SAN LORENZO, El Escorial Nuevos Museos. 470 × 206 cm.

The picture, which is signed and dated 1583, was brought from Italy in the year in which it was painted, together with Tintoretto's *Adoration of the Shepherds*. Both, according to an old and reliable tradition, were originally intended as a part of the main altar, but both were replaced. The Tintoretto was rejected because the figures were judged to be too small, but Veronese appears to have been given the wrong measurements since the *Nativity* by Pellegrino Tibaldi which replaced it was over a hundred centimetres shorter. Philip II was keen that the complex be painted by one artist commissioning first Federico Zuccaro, whose canvases were rejected, and then Pellegrino Tibaldi. The early sources refer to the Veronese with understandable admiration, and in this their judgement is preferable to the modern view which consigns it to the workshop (but how many critics have seen the altar to which the photo does less than justice?). No other Veronese is known to have been in Spain at this time and it must have influenced the decision in 1585 to approach Veronese to work at El Escorial instead of Federico Zuccaro (S. Saarrablo Aguareles, *Revista de Archivos, Bibliotecas y Museos*, 53, 1956, p. 663). The *Annunciation* from the Scuola dei Mercanti of 1577–78 (see under Plate 55) stood over a doorway which explains the emphasis upon the bravura architecture, which is repeated in the smaller version on the London market recently. The slighter figures and view of a building freely inspired by Sansovino's Library suggests an earlier date for the version in Lugano, while that in Cleveland is a simplified version of the El Escorial canvas.

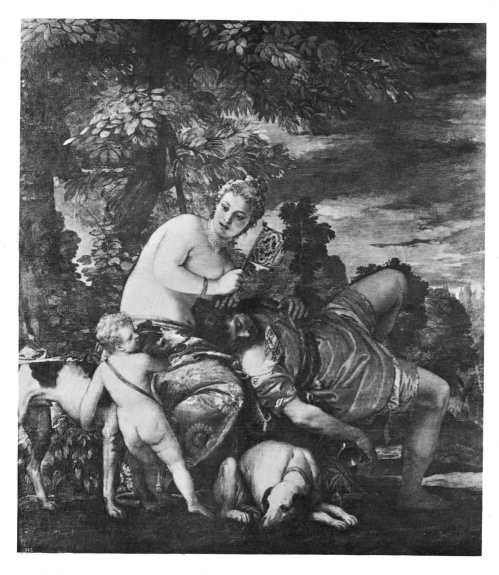

61 Venus and Adonis

MADRID, Museo del Prado. 212 × 191 cm.

This together with Plate 62 was one of the pair of paintings which in 1584 Veronese is reported as having just painted (specifically *not* for the Emperor Rudolph II) and which remained in Venice until they were acquired by Velazquez on his second visit to Italy in c. 1650; it was no. 595 in the Royal collection at the Alcázar in 1666. It is possible that the paintings were produced for stock and that they remained in the family collection like the slightly smaller *Venus and a Satyr* which had been painted by 1571. The earlier version in Augsburg, where the rich colour with the deep red of Adonis's robe set against the blue of the sky and the screen of trees that isolates the figures recall the 1573 *Rape* (Plate 41), reflects Titian's *poesie* for Philip II in the choice of moment with Adonis about to depart for the hunt. The idyllic mood of the Prado version reflects the illustrated editions of Ovid and contrasts with the coarseness, both in choice of moment and execution of the versions in Seattle and Vienna, by different members of the workshop.

VII Crucifixion

BUDAPEST, Museum der Bildenden Künste. 149 × 90 cm.

This marvellous late masterpiece, which the museum acquired from the Esterházy collection in 1871, links with Plate 57. It is the third non-narrative version by Veronese; the earliest is probably the undocumented side-altar in S. Sebastiano where the colour and the treatment of the figures is close to that of the lateral altars of 1565 (Plates 34 and 35). The Crucifixion in S. Lazzaro dei Mendicanti comes from the Ospedale degli Incurabili; work on the church recommenced in 1566, the likely date of this variation of Titian's Ancona altar. The Virgin's green and purple robes and St. John's red and yellow ones set against the dark skies may give an idea of the original colour of the much damaged 1574 *Lamentation* in Ostuni.

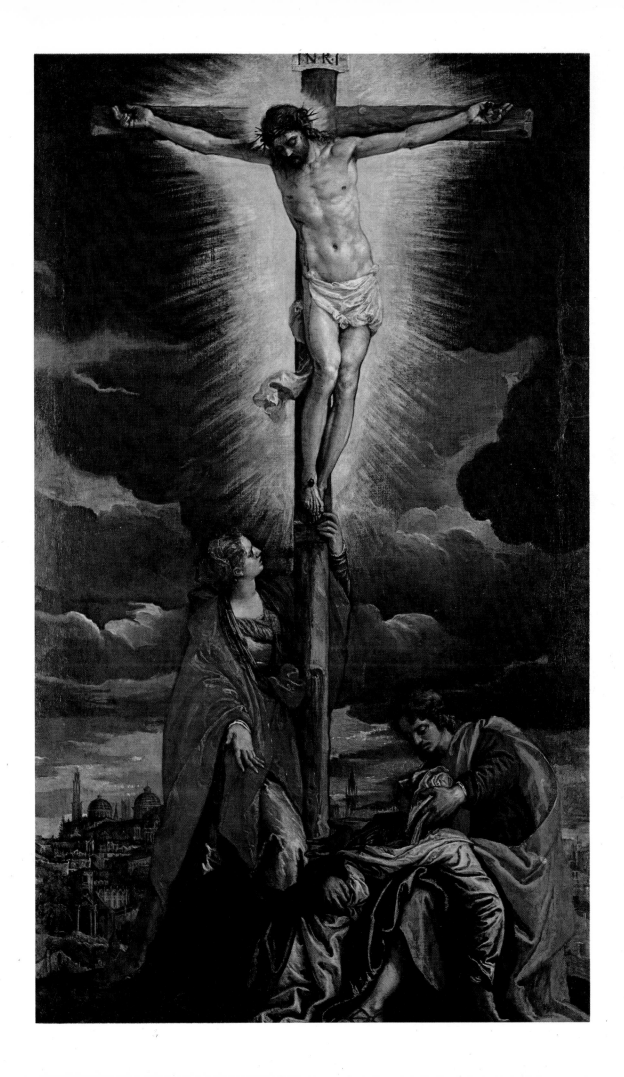

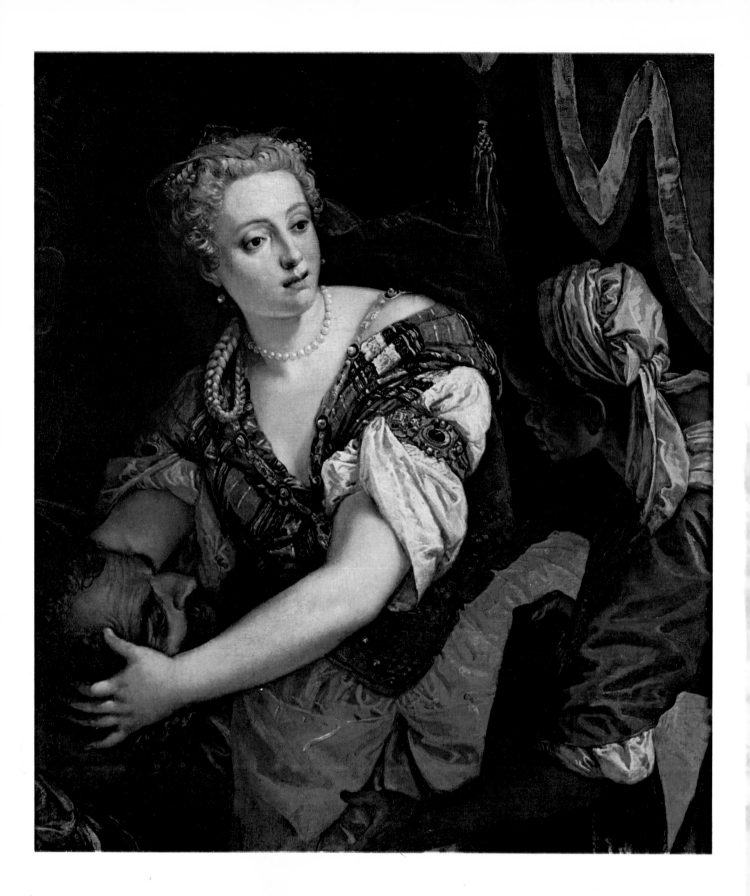

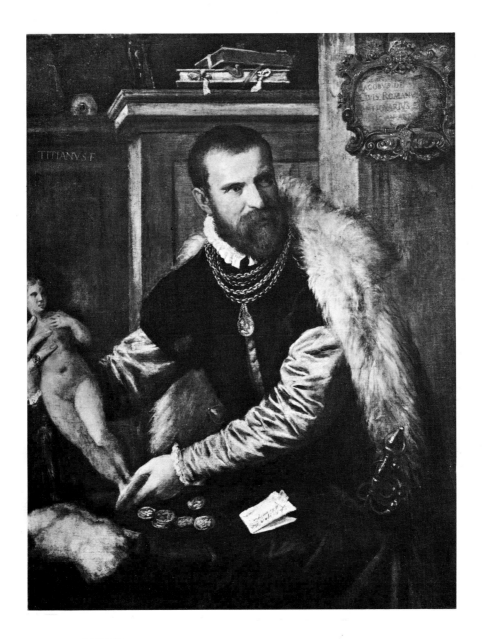

VIIIa TITIAN
Portrait of Jacopo Strada
VIENNA, Kunsthistorisches Museum.

VIII Judith

VIENNA, Kunsthistorisches Museum. 111 × 100.5 cm.

This marvellous late picture was first recorded in the collection of Archduke Leopold William in 1659, which formed the basis of the Vienna collections. The earliest version of this subject is that now in Genoa, which is badly rubbed but which must have been painted early in the 1560s since it inspired Zelotti's canvas of this subject on the ceiling of the Library at Praglia. The Genoa painting which may have been that offered for sale in Venice by Renier in 1666 (G 13 in the catalogue with dimensions of 11½ quarte by 11½, about 197 × 197 cm., very close to those of the Genoa canvas, 195 × 176) was seen in the Palazzo Balbi Genoa by de Seignelay in 1671 and in the Brignoletti Palace by Cochin in 1758. The choice of moment and the contrast between the figures reflect Mantegna's grisaille *Judith*; the Genoa painting was revised in the version in Caen one of four paintings of heroic women in the Bonaldi collection which, on the evidence of a drawing in the Hirsch collection (see M.D. 1973 pp. 141 ff.), were prepared in 1582, and which reveals an interest in Tintoretto's versions of the subject in the flickering torch-light. Like the other canvases of the series, which are autograph but which have suffered rubbing, cutting down and in the case of the *Rebecca* at Versailles enlargement, the Caen canvas is not well preserved and we can get some measure of what it has lost from the sparkling surface of this Vienna version.

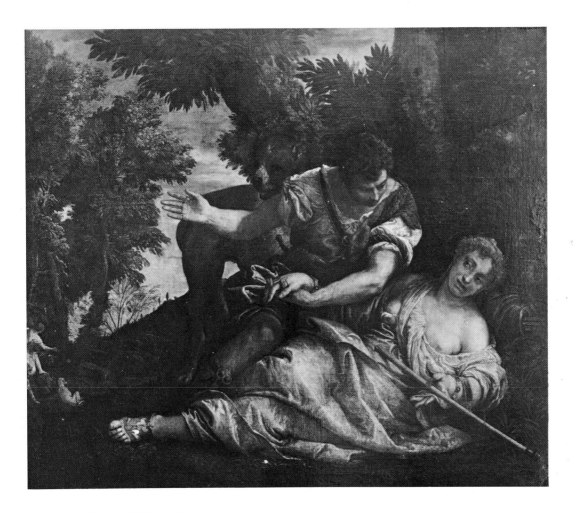

62 Cephalus and Procris

STRASBURG, Musée des Beaux-Arts. 162 × 190 cm.

The picture, the companion to Plate 61 which was cut down in the nineteenth century, had the same history as the *Venus and Adonis* probably being no. 601 in the 1666 inventory of the Alcázar where it remained until 1784. It was transferred to the Palacio de Buenvista in 1809 (see M. Lorente Junquera, *Archivo Espanol de Arte*, 1969, 235–243) and acquired by Joseph Bonaparte from whose collection it was sold, London 1845 and then again in 1851; it was acquired by the museum in 1912. The figures derive from those in the woodcut of this subject in the 1557 Lyons edition of Ovid (Plate 62) which may first have inspired the small version formerly in the Holford collection, London.

62a Death of Procris

La Metamorphose d'Ovide figurée, Lyons, 1557, f. 7v.

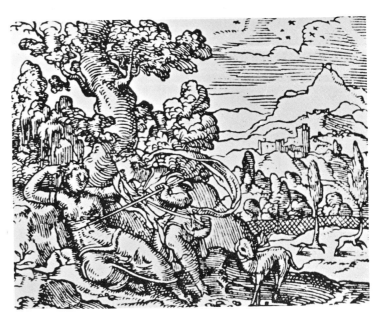

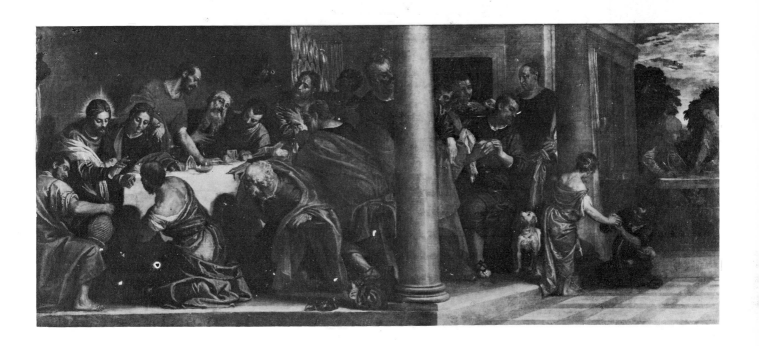

63 Last Supper

MILAN, Brera. 230 × 523 cm.

The picture, which was painted for S. Soffia, Venice and came to the museum in 1811, must have been painted by 1583 by which date the school produced a version for the Cappella del Santissimo, S. Giuliano which depends upon this painting. The oblique setting of the table, the response of the apostles and the bread given to the beggars link with Tintoretto's *Last Supper* in the Scuola Grande di S. Rocco of 1577–81 which breaks with the composition of his earlier *Last Suppers*. Both the Tintoretto in S. Rocco and the Veronese suggest as a distant model Taddeo Zuccaro's *Last Supper* in S. Maria della Consolazione, Rome, of 1556, the source of the twin columns that separate the Last Supper from the apostles' charitable work and of the oblique setting. Veronese has set the action in the foreground and is more concerned with the picture plane than Tintoretto; both the columns and the setting of the table link with the workshop *Marriage Feast at Cana* from S. Teonisto, Treviso of 1579–80. This could be the date of the Milan *Last Supper* which would thus have been painted at the same time as, and so independently of, the Tintoretto.

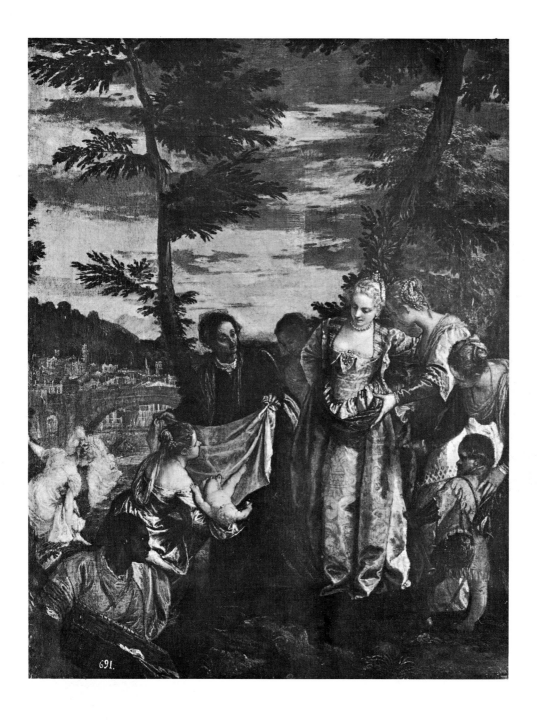

64   Finding of Moses

MADRID, Museo del Prado. 50 × 43 cm.

Charles I owned two small versions of this subject by Veronese; one which was bought from Daniel Nys in Venice in 1639 and was sold to Sir Peter Lely in 1650 (it measured 38 × 38 cm.); another with small figures was sold from his collection by Gravenor in 1649/50. It is not clear which was the present canvas which was probably no. 548 in the 1686 inventory of the Alcázar, where the dimensions fit with this canvas although the author is not specified. The other small canvas was sold from the collection of Pierre Crozat in 1751 and passed via a number of French owners to Catherine II of Russia in 1772; it was one of the paintings bought by Paul Mellon who gave it to the National Gallery, Washington. Veronese developed the subject from Bonifazio de' Pitati's *Finding* in Dresden with greater clarity in the contrast between the calm reflective Pharoah's daughter and the busy servants; and he appears to have produced a number of versions in a comparatively short time. I believe the prime canvas to be that in Dijon, usually classed as a school painting whose sombre dark tonality and landscape with a double vista which develops that of the *Rape* (Plate 41) suggest a date in the 1570s; it was followed by the Dresden and Lyons paintings and the Washington canvas.

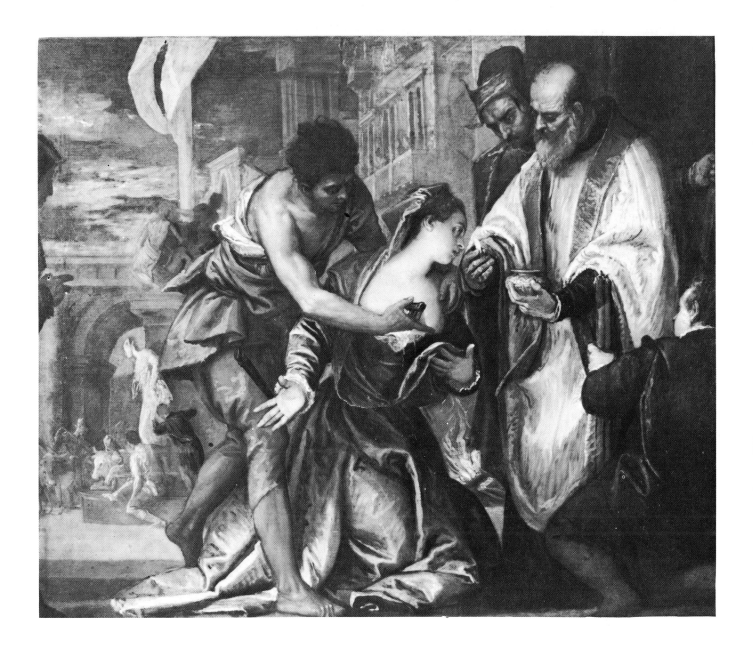

65 Last Communion and Martyrdom of St. Lucy

LONDON, Market (formerly). 137 × 173 cm.

This beautiful canvas, which has suffered some rubbing, was first recorded in the Lechi collection, Brescia in 1814 whence it was bought for Sir William Forbes of Fettercairn by 1827. It passed by descent until sold Christie 1971. The picture is one of those inspired by the *Golden Legend*, but, as noted in the text, the emphasis upon the priest with the chalice and the host is very different from that in the earlier version by Altichiero, a change that may well reflect the influence of the Tridentine re-affirmation of the worship of the host. This belief also influenced the *Virgin and Child Appear to St. Luke* in S. Luca where the appearance of the angel with the host is without precedent.

66 Coronation of the Virgin

VENICE, Accademia. 396 × 219 cm.

This picture which is an outstanding example of Veronese's adaptation of Tintoretto's light effects, was painted for the main altar of Ognisanti which, together with the church, was consecrated on 21 July 1586. The preparatory drawings for the canvas, in Oxford and Berlin, contain motifs that are re-used in the Lille *modello* for the *Paradise* in the Sala del Gran Consiglio which dates from after 1584 and before 1587 (when Bardi notes that it was to have been undertaken with Francesco Bassano) and which confirm the date of the present canvas as 1585–86. The inspiration for this fusion of the *Coronation* with an *All Saints* must have come from its location on the altar of Ognisanti (All Saints) and the attendant saints are developed from Titian's *Gloria* of 1554 which had earlier inspired the drawings of the *Allegory of Redemption* now in the Metropolitan Museum while the group of the Virgin, Christ and God the Father are inspired by Dürer's engraving of the *Assumption and Coronation of the Virgin.*

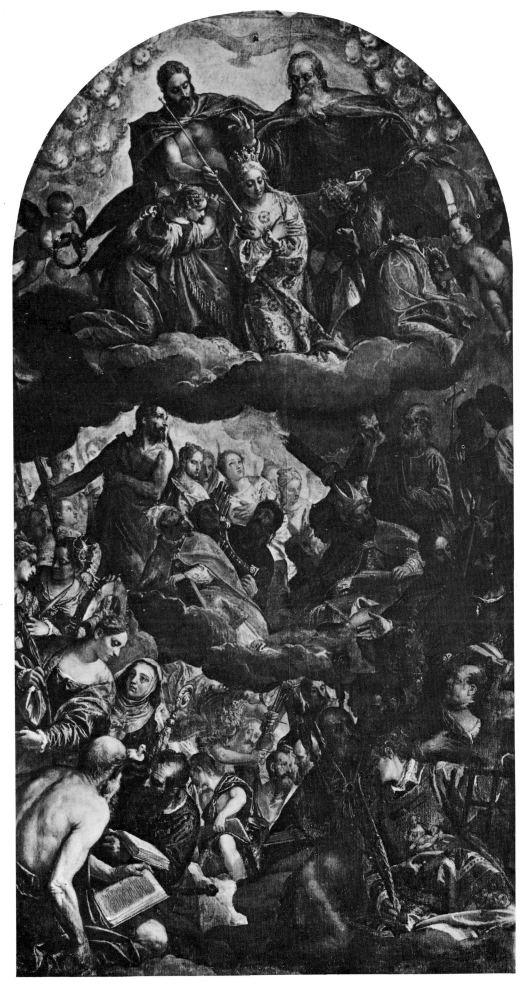

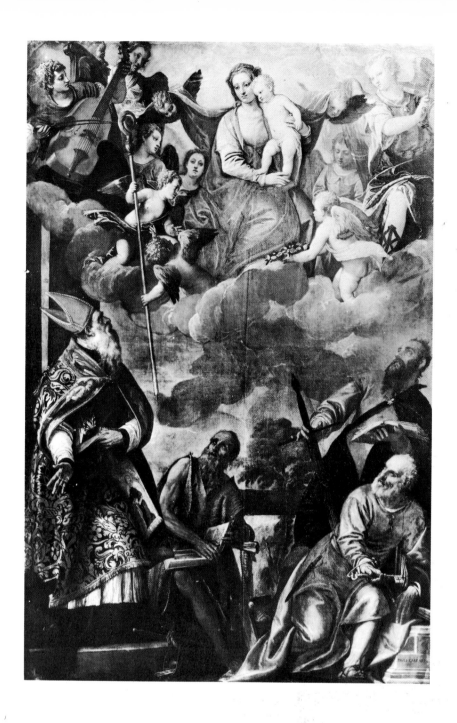

67   Virgin and Child Appear to SS. Anthony Abbot, Paul the Hermit, Peter and Paul

DIJON, Musée des Beaux-Arts. 341 × 219 cm.

The picture, which was painted for the Confraternity of St. Anthony, Pesaro in 1586, was removed to France in 1799 and sent to Dijon in 1809. The execution of the picture, to which the photograph does less than justice, is usually given to the workshop; comparison of the St. Anthony on the left of this painting with the St. Frediano in Carletto's *Virgin and Child Appear to the Magdalen St. Frediano, an Unidentified Saint and a Donor* in the Uffizi (Plate 67a) reveals that the St. Frediano is flat and badly drawn and his drapery has none of the depth or life that makes St. Anthony's so exciting and convincing. There is a problem about St. Anthony's appearance in a rich brocade and bishop's mitre looking up to the skies where the angels carry a bishop's staff; St. Anthony was famous as a hermit (see Plate 28) and although he can be shown in a sacra conversazione as in Plate 3 accompanied by his pig the accoutrements and action suggest some special event within the Confraternity. On the 28 May 1586 Caesar de Benedictis, about whom little is known except that he was a priest in Pesaro, became the city's new Bishop; it seems possible that he was the member of the Confraternity whose elevation inspired the imagery of this painting, for which Veronese received payment on 31st of May.

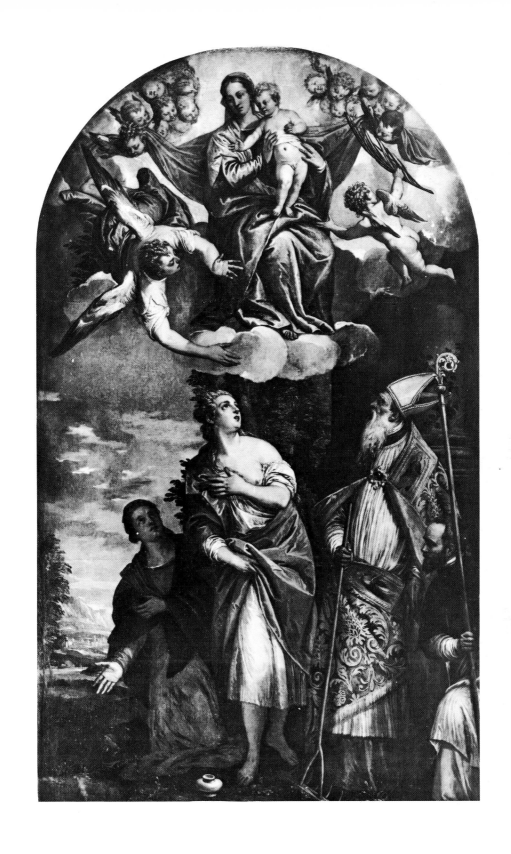

67a CARLETTO CALIARI
Virgin and Child Appear to the Magdalen St. Frediano, an Unidentified Saint and a Donor
FLORENCE, Galleria Uffizi.

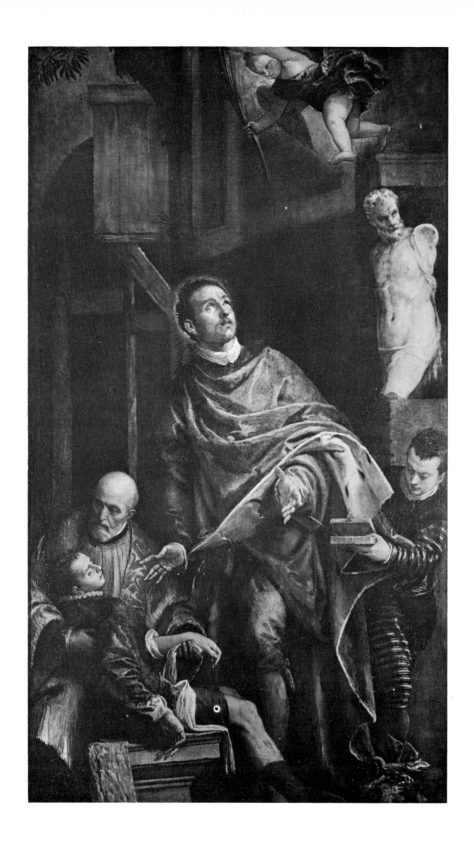

68 St. Pantaleon Heals a Sick Boy

VENICE, S. Pantaleone. 277 × 160 cm.

This splendidly preserved painting was commissioned by Bartolommeo Borghi, who is shown holding the boy whom the saint heals, in 1587. It was originally on the high altar of the church which was rebuilt between 1668 and 1686 and it was removed to its present site, where it is very difficult to see, on the second altar on the right of the nave in 1773.

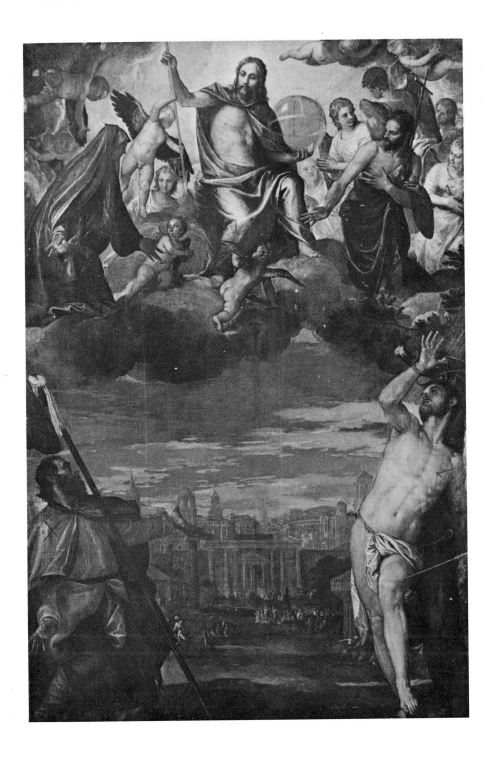

69 The Deësis with SS. Sebastian and Roch

ROUEN, Musée des Beaux-Arts. 340 × 220 cm.

This, one of the most moving and personal of all Veronese's altars, was painted for the main altar of S. Rocco, Parma from where it was removed at the orders of Napoleon in 1796 and was sent to Rouen in 1801. The church was given to the Jesuits in 1564, at which date it was not roofed; this was completed as a response to the plague of 1572. The main chapel was extended by 1578 and the altar built in 1589 although work continued until 1598. The activity in the centre of the canvas suggests an idealized picture of the church being built. The kneeling St. Roch is similar to the *St. Roch* in Cividale, one of two paintings commissioned in 1584. There can be no doubt that the companion *Virgin and Child in Glory* is from the workshop; the *St. Roch*, which is signed (as are many clearly workshop paintings) is, to judge from a reproduction (the painting having been stolen from the church in 1973), possibly autograph.

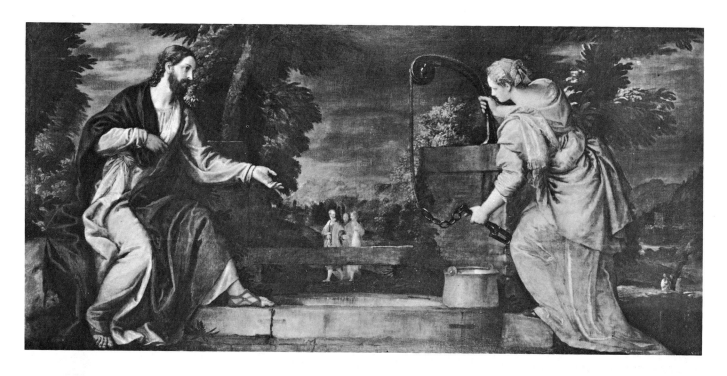

70 Christ with the Woman of Samaria

VIENNA, Kunsthistorisches Museum. 143 × 289 cm.

This is one of a series of ten canvases with scenes from the Old and New Testament which were first mentioned in the 1635 inventory of the 2nd Duke of Buckingham (see Davies, B.M., 1906–07, p. 380) and were in his sale, Antwerp in 1648 and then in the Austrian Imperial collection where they were first inventoried in Prague in 1721. The other autograph paintings (although there is an enormous range of critical opinion) are: the *Rebecca and Eliezer* in Washington, the *Angel Appears to Hagar and Ishmael* in Vienna and the *Christ Washing the Apostles Feet* in Prague. The preparatory drawing in Cassel for this latter painting includes on its recto sketches for a painting by Gabriele Caliari (see M.D. 1973 p. 145) which, since he was born in c. 1568, confirms a late date for the series. The remaining six canvases, which with the exception of the Prague *Adoration of the Shepherds* are all in Vienna, were completed by different hands in the workshop. With the exception of the Prague *Adoration*, which suggests Veronese's supervision, there is a contrast in quality and in the viewpoint. The five school paintings in Vienna were intended to be hung high, perhaps because of a change of plan or because the workshop had some new information about the location of the series.

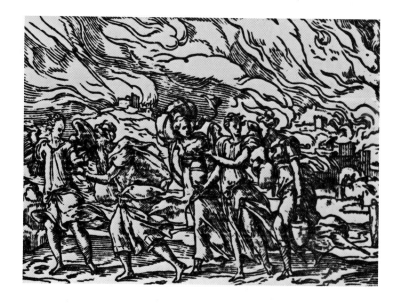

71a The Flight of Loth

B. Saloman, *Quadrins historiques de la Bible*, Lyon, 1555, Genesis XIX.

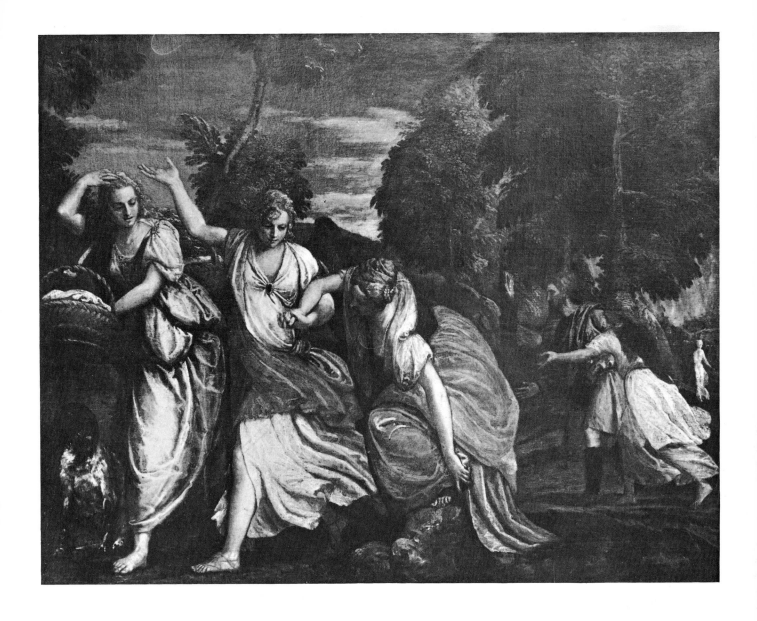

71 The Flight of Loth

PARIS, Musée du Louvre. 92 × 130 cm.

This small canvas, which was first recorded in the Orléans collection in 1727, was not sold with
the rest of the collection at the end of the century but was acquired for the Galerie du Musée
Napoleon by 1815. As with many late Veronese's it has suffered and it has obvious weaknesses in
the gesture of the daughter to the left raising her hand to her head and in the relationship of the
angel's left foot to the body; but the swirling draperies create a sense of movement and drama
which is beyond the workshop and I therefore believe it to be a late autograph work which
inspired the clumsier version from the Duke of Buckingham's collection now in Vienna, where this
sense of movement and excitement is lost in the unsuccessful search for solid forms. The initial
inspiration for the composition may have come from the woodcut of this subject (Genesis XIX) is
Salomon's *Quadrins* published in Lyon in 1555 (Plate 71a), although a comparison reveals the extent to
which Veronese has reworked his source. The other workshop paintings in Vienna from the Duke of
Buckingham's collection also depend upon slightly earlier Veronese's; the *Esther* is an unintelligent
transformation of the Bonaldi version now in the Louvre; the *Susanna* fuses elements from the
versions in the Louvre (again a Bonaldi commission) and the Prado; the *Sacrifice of Isaac* fails to fill
out the smaller upright version of this subject (inspired by Titian's ceiling formerly in S. Spirito)
now in the Prado.

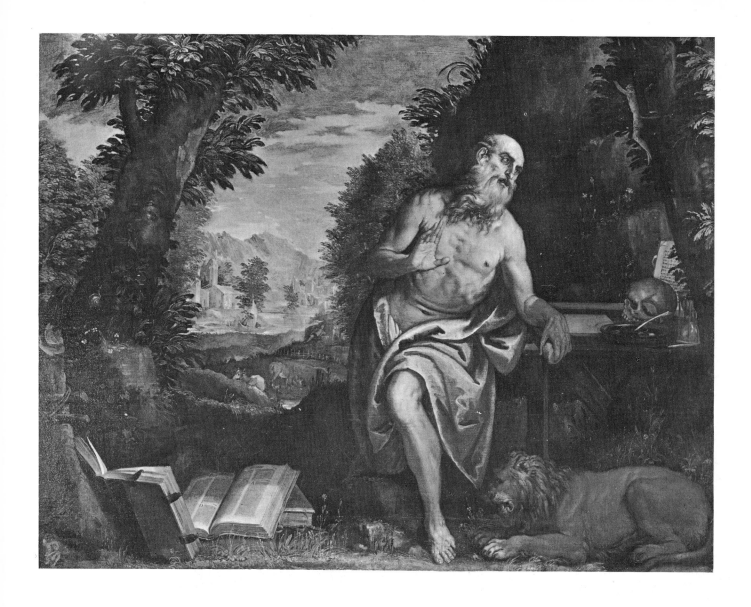

72 St. Jerome

CHICAGO, Art Institute. 135.3 × 176.6 cm.

The picture was acquired in Florence by the Reverend John Sanford in the 1830s and was in his sale in 1839 (see Nicolson, B.M. 1955, p. 214); subsequently it was in the collection of the Earl of Stafford, thence to A. L. Nicholson in 1932 and donated to the museum in 1947. The saint is handled with the athletic assurance of the version in Murano of 1567 but the fussy details in the landscape where cows graze and a boat sails in front of the church are very different from Veronese's backgrounds and connect with that in which Carletto placed his *Penitent Magdalen* (Plate 72a), formerly at Alnwick. X-rays confirm that the saint was painted first, by Veronese, and that the landscape was then added, by Carletto. The saint's contrapposto is developed from that of the slightly earlier *S. Jerome* now in S. Andrea, Venice, which reflects Jacopo Bassano's *St. Jerome* of c. 1570 in the Accademia. The setting in the S. Andrea painting, with the flight of stairs leading to an obelisk may have a meaning that evades us, especially since the painting, which was first mentioned in S. Andrea in 1648, was probably not painted for the church. One other canvas was finished by the workshop, the *Adoration of the Shepherds* in S. Giuseppe, where the St. Jerome and the Virgin and Child on the left are autograph, but the shepherds on the right are the work of the studio.